To: Sharon

God Bless you!

Kay Williams

0

Through The Eyes Of Grace

D1525337

By: Kay E. Williams

Table Context

Table Context cont.

Table Context cont.

Introduction

Have you ever struggled with your faith? Have you ever felt ashamed or felt like you even hit rock bottom? Grace in this story has been through most of this in her life. Through the eyes of Grace is based on true inspiring events. This inspiring story of a girl named Grace will take you on a journey through every experience she's been in throughout her life. Grace has suffered many losses and hardships in her life. This story is to encourage that we all go through pain and suffering with struggles beyond what we can handle throughout our lives. We may even have experienced loss at one point in our lives; however no matter our struggles or situations we go through in life we are never alone and we can find hope in Jesus. Grace went through a lot of traumatic experiences throughout her life and struggled with her faith in the Lord. She faced many difficult decisions but no matter what she faced in life even

when she didn't realize at the time, God was always
by her side. That is how unconditional love works.
God sees our struggles; he is just waiting for us to
cry out to him so he can begin to heal us from the
inside and out. What does it mean when you put it
all together? It means that Jesus Christ took our
place. He took the curse of our sins for us. He paid a
debt in full at the cross so that we may live a
healthier and better, peaceful lifestyle according to
his word. He was pierced because of us, and for us.
No man on Earth can endure the pain and suffering
that Jesus went through. This is true unconditional
love. Through the eyes of Grace explains to readers
that everyone has a past and every Christian
struggles with their faith at some point in their lives
as Grace did throughout hers. She also struggles
with learning to love and how to be loved. We know
as christians that God is love and love comes from
God. Grace had to learn for herself.   Whether or
not she chooses to stay in the past or move forward
from it is entirely up to her. Grace is on a long
Journey of really understanding her faith. It's a

battle between the spirit and the flesh and as Paul says in

(Romans 8:5-6) "For those who live according to the flesh set their minds on the things of the flesh, but those who live according to the spirit, set their minds on the things of the spirit. For to be carnally minded is death, but to be spiritually minded is life and peace."

Throughout Grace's life she would have to eventually learn how to find her faith by walking in the spirit. How does she find her faith you ask? That's an answer for what lies ahead. God points her in the direction but does she follow? The choice would be entirely up to her. When we don't know which way to go, always look up and follow the one who brings new life, and new beginnings. Jesus will set us on the right path if we choose to follow his instructions, which can always be found in the Holy Bible.

(Hebrews 12:2) "Looking unto Jesus, the author and finisher of our faith, who for the joy that was set before him

endured the cross, despising the shame, and has sat down at the right hand of the throne of God."

God is in this story and he is and always will be the author and finisher of this story. This story is for his glory. I want to take a moment to just pray for whoever is reading this right now. My prayer for you: Father God let this book inspire those who have had struggles with faith in their life or throughout their life. Let it touch every heart that has been broken from the many sorrows of this world. Help each and every person to move forward from their past and help them to overcome their past. Jesus you are indeed the author and finisher of this story and our faith. Bless every heart and guide them through their journey of faith, Father God. Let this book encourage others to want to get to know your Son Jesus who shed his blood just to save us from our own destruction because of our sins. Again I ask that you bless every person reading this story today, let it be an encouragement to others. In Jesus name, Amen!

Chapter 1
Cherished Memories

Have you ever felt alone and scared in this world you may not understand? It's not always easy when you feel all alone and scared in a big world. We're not really alone because the presence of the Lord is here all around us when we take the time to have faith and just believe in his word. His word is truth and teaches us how to live and survive in this fallen world.   According to the bible we are not alone even when we do feel like we are scared and lonely in this broken world.

(Isaiah 41:10) says "Do not fear, for I am with you; neither be dismayed, for I am your God. I will strengthen you and help you; I will uphold you with my righteous hand."

So again we are not really alone are we? Allow me to introduce myself, my name is Grace Emilia Lockwood.   This is my story about how Jesus my Lord and savior changed my life. He changed my way of thinking. Every situation he brought me out of, He helped get me through them. I grew up in Cleveland Ohio where I spent most of my early childhood, living with my grandparents, grandpa Clay and grandma Asa Lockwood. Most of my life I was in and out of the christian church. But First; I want to start at the beginning of my story. I never did know my father or much about him, except that he was from South America and lives in Florida. My mother Mary Kay Atkins was married to my brother's father. She had my brother Adam Bradley Atkins first before she had me. Adam was born in Jacksonville Florida 1986. One year later she divorced Adam's father. She met my father a few years later. Then got pregnant again, then left the state of Florida. She took a plane back to Cleveland Ohio where she met up with my grandma Asa and had me at Franklin Memorial hospital on the Eastside of Cleveland. I was born 3 years after Adam. It was the year of 1989 when I was born. It was a cold winter that year in December. My mother decided to stay with my grandparents because she had nowhere else to go after the divorce with Adam's father. My grandma Asa picked my mother and I up from the hospital christmas Eve morning, 2 days after the day I was born. Adam had stayed with my grandparents at the time of my birth while my mother and I were still in the hospital. My mom was now officially a single mother of 2 kids. She was struggling to find work so she decided to go back to school and try to get her LPN. We stayed with my grandparents for a long time. My mother wasn't around as much. Her focus was on school, and finding a job to help support us. The hospital called my mother one morning. They told her she had to bring me to Rainbow babies and children's hospital, and that it was urgent that she bring me right away. So when we arrived at the main lobby of the hospital she met with Doctor Sue Jackson. She explained to my mother that one of the tests that they did at Franklin Memorial Hospital came back positive so they wanted to transfer me to University Hospitals in downtown Cleveland and keep me for a little while to perform tests and observations on me.

A month went by and my mother got the news from Doctor Sue Jackson that I was diagnosed with an incurable disease called Phenylketonuria that can be treated with medication and a very strict diet for the rest of my life. Phenylketonuria is an inherited inability to metabolize phenylalanine that causes brain damage and nerve damage if untreated or not treated properly. My mom felt depressed and confused when she heard the news then she called grandma Asa and told her what she was just told by the doctor. Then grandpa Clay also over heard grandma talking to my mom over the phone about the diagnosis, he was completely surprised about it and made a promise to grandma that he'd make sure I'd have my medicine and the right care that I need. Grandpa Clay always said Adam and I were very special to him and grandma. They too were also special to me and my brother Adam.

(Psalm 103:17) "But from everlasting to everlasting the Lord's love is with those who fear him, and his righteousness with their children's children."

God's love is everlasting and can be passed down
through generation after generation. As days moved
on Adam and I enjoyed our time living with grandpa
Clay and grandma Asa. Adam sometimes went with
our mother to school cause they had a daycare at the
college she was going to. Mom and grandma
enrolled him in a preschool program at Kennedy
Elementary on East 155th street. Grandma Asa
would sometimes volunteer her services at the
school. I was just a baby at the time so I stayed
home with grandpa Clay since I was too much of a
handful to go to the childcare at my mother's
college. If I wasn't with my grandpa Clay I would
have temper tantrums like crying, screaming and
yelling, but when I was with grandpa Clay I was
calm and happy. Adam and I used to have fun
watching old western movies that were in black and
white television with grandpa Clay. The fun
memories were when we used to go on walks
through the metro parks with grandpa Clay to enjoy
all the wildlife and nature scenery. We would walk

around the duck pond exploring God's creation with the different kind of wildlife animals.

(Genesis 1:21) "So God created the great sea creatures and every living creature that moves, according to their kinds, and every winged bird according to its kind, and God saw that it was good.

Grandpa Clay also used to take us to different parks around Cleveland and we'd have fun playing on the playground at Sims park, or swinging on tires at the tire park, in Euclid. Grandpa Clay used to work for the railroad company called Conrail. After he retired he would take us up to the railroad station and show us around to introduce us to all the people he used to work with. Grandpa Clay would also take Adam and I to the cinemark movie theaters down the street. He'd take us during the day where tickets were only one dollar and at night time it was $1.50. On Tuesdays it was only 50 cents all day. Times with grandma Asa were filled with a lot of loving and joyful memories. Grandma never got out much; she stayed home a lot and did indoor and outdoor work. Working in the garden with grandma Asa was a delight. I used to help her plant some of her favorite flowers in the garden. Grandma's favorite flowers were pansies and marigolds. Sometimes grandma would sit on her porch swing and smoke a cigarette or 2 while watching me and my brother play on the swing set her and grandpa bought for us on one christmas morning. Grandma and grandpa didnt have a lot of money back then. We grew up in a poor neighborhood. We still managed to get by through times of hardship. We still managed to find things to do without worrying about spending money on things.

(1 Timothy 6:10) "For the love of money is the root of all kinds of evils. It is through this craving that some have wandered away from the faith and pierced themselves with many pangs."

They had to save up for a few months just so they could get the things Adam and I needed and eventually my mother got a job so she can help support us as well. Mother was working hard to get back on her feet again but the divorce from when she was married to Adam's dad was really rough on her mentally and physically.   Grandma and Grandpa did a lot for us out of love and through the kindness in their heart.

(Ephesians 4:32) says "Be kind to each other, tenderhearted, forgiving one another, just as God through Christ has forgiven you."

In my opinion I felt in my heart our grandparents were trying to be a good example of that verse. Although they were far from perfect, they still tried their best to be that example through the eyes of the good Lord. In my heart I always seemed to know that the Lord was always with me but in my mind I didn't seem to realize that. I had a lot of memories of me and my brother going to church with grandpa and grandma. The church our grandparents took us to was called Nottingham United Methodist Church on St. Clair Ave in East Cleveland. The church was only a few blocks down.   Adam and I joined a youth ministry called Cleveland Praise Ministry.   We learned about how to be a clown in a loving christian way. My brother Adam preferred to dress up as a clown. That just wasn't my thing. We learned gospel music in sign language. Then my favorite was learning how to be a puppeteer. We learned how to use the puppets to sing songs, and do skits in spreading God's love through the creative art of puppetry.

(Exodus 35:31-33) "And he has filled him with the Spirit of God, with skill, with intelligence, with knowledge and with all craftsmanship, to devise artistic designs, to work in gold, silver and bronze, in cutting stones for setting, and in carving wood, for work in every skilled craft."

Those whom God called by name to his service, he filled with His Spirit. God gave us the supernatural ability to operate through the work of art, on His behalf in producing good fruit within the purpose of God. One of the best memories was going on tours to different churches all across the United States to spread God's love through our type of Evangilisic ministry. Evangelism is the spreading of the gospel through ministry or personal witness. This was the first time I felt closer with God through a divine connection with Him. It was throughout this ministry that I felt the spiritual connection with God. Before that took place my grandma Asa used to be in girl scouts through the church. We always tried to go on a regular basis. When my grandma met up with the girl scout group, she'd bring me sometimes. That's where I met my friend Shantel. She was in girl scouts with her mom. She also joined the Cleveland Praise Ministry team with us. She decided puppetry wasn't her thing so she preferred to clown around with my brother Adam. She too went on tours and traveled around with us spreading God's love everywhere we went. We had a lot of fun together with Cleveland Praise Ministry. We were in this ministry for a long time. Shantel and I were close friends growing up. We used to go play behind the church at the playground they had for us kids during Sunday school or after church. Her mom was good friends with my grandma Asa. Shantel and I also went to Sunday school together. They went to church every Sunday her and her mom. We didn't go that much cause grandma and grandpa didn't always have the motivation or the energy to go every Sunday. In Sunday school when did go almost regularly, we learned about scripture.

(John 3:16) "For God so loved the world he gave his one and only son to die for our sins, and whosoever believes in him shall have eternal life."

They taught us a lot of things in Sunday school like learning about forgiveness, love, joy and peace. Holidays at the church was always fun they had lots of activities for us kids like watching a Mickey Mouse Christmas Carol, they had arts and crafts, games with prizes and even Santa Claus.   Holidays with the family was also fun too. I came from a big family. Our family didn't always get along with one another, of course that's most families these days. Growing up I always clinged to my grandpa Clay since I never had anyone around to call dad. He was like a father to me. I remember when he would rock me to sleep in his old rocking chair or read stories to me and my brother Adam before bedtime and the baby blanket that my grandma made for me with love.   It was as white as snow and so soft I cuddled with it all the time, and took it with me everywhere I went. I have so many fun memories with my grandparents like the times when they took us to Euclid beach where we went swimming in Lake Erie. There was a time when my grandpa took me to this camp that was recommended by doctor Sue Jackson. It was a camp with other kids who shared the same medical condition as me. I got to really learn more about myself everytime I went to that camp. I had gotten really close with my doctor's and made friends with other campers that shared the same disease as me. We were like a big family having fun singing campfire songs, horseback riding, going swimming, and other fun camp activities. I often looked forward to camp even though it was once a year. Grandpa Clay always took me to camp. Then I remembered the times when grandpa Clay took us to go see my cousin David play baseball. My brother Adam and I would play at the playground during the baseball games with our other cousins. When I used to play softball grandpa Clay would be at every game always cheering me on. He took me and my brother to a Cleveland Indians game once. We had so many fun memories at the baseball games. I remember that time when Adam and I went to our first christian concert with grandma Asa and grandpa Clay to see the Gathers live and in person. Even though at that time I didnt understand the meaning behind the music. The music felt peaceful and a joy to my heart. I cherished a lot of these memories for a long time even till this day.

(Psalm 92:14) "They will still bear fruit in old age, they will stay fresh and green."

Even though my grandparents didn't go to church every Sunday like Shantel and her mom, my grandparents still had their faith in Jesus. They have different ways of serving the Lord outside of church. Yeah my grandparents had their flaws and Lord knows I had mine even as a child. They seemed to be perfectly imperfect, but made perfect through God's eyes.

(Romans 15:7) "Therefore welcome one another as Christ has welcomed you, for the glory of God.

Though not all of us are perfect, yes we make mistakes, that's why the Lord guides us through the good and the bad things. Christ accepts you as is, flaws and all. He doesn't require your perfection, because he is the only one who can be completely without sin. His acceptance of you can help you accept others with their flaws as well. God didnt create us to figure things out on our own. God asks us to trust Him, read our bible, pray, and seek Godly wisdom. This story is just getting started, it's only just the beginning of my journey of faith.

Chapter 2
The Start of A Broken Spirit

In the year of 1993 my mom got remarried to a guy named Mark Saunders. She then had the last name Saunders now. Mine and my brother's last name remained the same. Eventually our mother moved us out of our grandparents house because we now shared a house with Mark on the westside of Cleveland. We first stayed in an apartment with Mark on Denison Ave. Mark and mom bought a house together on Riverdale off of West 25th in the year of 1994. I spent most of my life living on the westside. Mark also used to work at Cleveland Hopkins airport. My mother would take Adam and I sometimes up at the airport just so we could see Mark. I didn't always like doing things or going places with my mother. One time my mom nd her friend tried to take Adam and I somewhere, but I would just scream and cry. I missed my grandpa

Clay all the time. I was so used to the way things were for the longest time living with Grandpa Clay and grandma Asa. Mark was fun to be around. Soon enough Adam and I started to call him daddy. Our mother told Mark about my disease and Mark vowed to always take care of me and my brother. He loved us very much and we loved him too. Mark tried to do anything and everything for me and my brother Adam.

(1 Corinthians 13:7) says that "Love bears all things, Believes all things, hopes all things, endures all things." Although Mark may not have seemed perfect, he was to Adam and I. He still tried his best to help our mother raise and support us. He was the dad I never had. Mark was a christian man raised up at St. James Lutheran church where me and my brother Adam were first baptized at. We also attended Sunday school classes there too. We had fun singing songs on the sunday school bus. Mark played basketball at the church. He took Adam and I with him a lot when he played up there with his friends from the church. Adam and I would just play on the

jungle gym while he played. My mom used to watch him play as she would cheer him on in the bleachers. Mark also played baseball in the adult leagues. Our mother would take us to Mark's games, as we'd go to and run off to the playground while he plays. Mark and my mom used to bowl together on a bowling league. Mark was very active in sports. Adam and I would be in the childrens nursery while Mark and my mom bowled for hours. The nursery was always fun. They had lots of toys and other kids that would come play and have fun with us. The nursery workers also used to play games with us like red rover or doggy where's your bone, and even Simon says. As the years flew by my mom got pregnant again with my sister Ruth Ann Saunders. I was so excited about having a sister that I wanted to be the best big sister I could be to her.

(Proverbs 3:15) says "She is more precious than jewels, and nothing you desire can compare with her."

I loved my sister so much that I wanted to do everything with her. I thanked God in my heart that I became a big sister. I wondered sometimes of how

I could help my mom with her. I could assist my mother when she needs to change her or help make her warm bottles or even share my toys with her. Adam seemed pleased to have two sisters now. Just when I had thought things were going great there came a turning point in my life where things aren't always as they seemed. For instance one day I found out Mark actually had another daughter by a previous marriage. Her name was Lynn Michelle Saunders, she was 16 years old when her mom just dropped her off at our doorstep. Her mom gave Mark the responsibility of raising her. Lynn was a troubled young teenager. I thought having 2 sisters might be fun but it wasn't. Lynn babysat me, my brother, and Ruth a lot so mom and Mark could go out and have time for themselves. One time Lynn even locked me in our dark and creepy basement while we were playing hide and go seek. She thought it was so funny. I'm not gonna lie, I seemed to hate her after that. She got me in trouble once with Mark, she told him I was messing with his stereo system when actually it was my mom trying to play music on Mark's stereo. I got back handed in the mouth for no reason but, Mark didn't stay mad at me he got mad at my mom when he found out it was her that played with his stereo. That was Mark's biggest rule in the house: do not touch the stereo system. Mark loved us very much. For sometime I didnt think Mark loved me anymore ever since I got punished for not touching his stereo system. I cried a lot when I was younger because I missed my grandpa Clay all the time. Lynn was always mean to me. She watched me when everyone else was gone in their busy day. Mark was at work during the day at the airport. Adam was always playing with his friend next door. Ruth was always doing something with mom. I just stayed in the living room watching tv most of the time while Lynn was on the phone or listening to music on her cd player. I became a depressed little girl feeling ignored and unloved most of the time.

(John 16:33) "I have told you these things, so that in me you may have peace. In this world you will have trouble, But take heart, I have overcome the world."

The Lord says we will go through troubles in this world but He said take heart Jesus overcame the world. We can trust in Jesus at all times in anything. He'll be there to comfort us in our time of great need. I used to have separation anxiety from not being with my grandpa Clay. My mom and Mark started getting into a lot of arguments all the time. Sometimes it would get physical so Adam called grandpa Clay and he would have to come get us when it got out of control, but that was fine by me as long as I got to be with my grandpa Clay. At this time I never knew how or why the arguments happened, I just was too young to understand. I remember grandpa shouting at my mother to get her to calm down when she seemed so angry. When she'd get into it with Mark she'd get louder and louder. I got really scared when mom threw a hairdryer at Mark from the top of the staircase and Mark got mad and ran upstairs after her. I remember Mark grabbing some bags and walking out the door one day. He left and stayed with his friend Tom for a little while. We'd still hear from Mark on the phone. He'd tell me and Adam how much he loved us and how he misses all of us. I remember him crying on the phone one day which made Adam and I cry just by listening to the sound of his voice while tears were being shed. He said he wanted things to work out with him and our mother so we could go back to being a family again.

(Isaiah 40:31) says "But those who hope in the Lord will renew their strength. They will soar on wings like eagles; they will run and not grow weary, they will walk and not faint."

There is always hope in Jesus for everything. Mom had talked with Mark on the phone at times trying to set aside the littles things so they could work on their relationship. It was 1997 I was in the 2nd grade. Adam was in 5th grade at the time. We were both sent to the principal's office while worried, as if we did something wrong. We just heard the news from our principal and office staff at the school that Mark had a heart attack in his sleep. He was found dead in bed at his friend Tom's house. Tom noticed he was dead when he tried to wake him up and Mark was unresponsive, so he called 911. When they came to Tom's house they pronounced him dead at that time since he had no vitals and his heart was stopped. So many thoughts, feelings of mixed emotions were running right through me I didn't know how to respond to such horrifying news that my daddy Mark was dead. I felt scared, lonely and more depressed. In the bible the Lord says

(Joshua 1:9) "Have I not commanded you? Be strong and courageous, do not be afraid; do not be discouraged, for the Lord your God will be with you wherever you go."

God tells us to be strong when things get rough, but sadly at this time I had no strength, I became very weak in spirit. Adam and I have grown so close to Mark over the years we didn't take this news very well. Grandpa Clay always said you'll see him again someday but I didn't understand what that meant yet. All I could think is that my daddy Mark was gone and that he wasn't coming back.

(John 16:22) says "So also you will have sorrow now: but I will see you again, and your hearts will rejoice, and no one will take your joy from you."

God wants us to understand that we will all be reunited with him one day in his kingdom. I didn't have any joy at this time all I felt was pain and hurt. I was too young to understand anything that was going on. I just wanted God to take the pain away. This was one of the many painful sorrows that lie ahead.

Chapter 3
The Process of Grieving

Enduring a loss is likely the most challenging thing we as humans face in life. There are 3 stages of grief number 1 is avoidance. Avoidance means being in the sense of disbelief or in complete shock at the news of the loss of a loved one. Number 2 is Confrontation. Confrontation means a time of readjustment, during the reality that a loved one is gone and becomes harder to ignore. During this stage of grieving the reminders of loss can be very painful and frequent. In this particular part of the process of grieving a person is reminded time and time again that their loved one is no longer here, that their spirit has left this realm. This can leave a person confused and conflicted. Stage number 3 is the last stage out of the 3 called accommodation. Accommodation means a person coming to terms with their loss of a loved one and starts to have a more spiritual connection with the deceased. Its a slow process of moving forward in life.

(Psalm 34:18) says "The Lord is near to the brokenhearted and saves the crushed in spirit."

The Lord is always near us even when we don't see it. He comforts us even when we don't feel it. As my story continues it fell in November of 1997. The month and year of Mark's death. A few days later we were all getting ready to go to Mark's funeral. My mom puts me in nice dress clothes for the funeral. The funeral home was called Wilson and Sons funeral home on Clark Avenue. On the way to the funeral home I couldn't stop crying and staring out the window with this sad depressed look on my face like all hope was lost.

(Psalm 73:26) "My flesh and my heart faileth: but God is the strength of my heart, and my portion forever."

God is our strength in our time of sorrow. He will lift us up when we choose to keep our eyes on him and not the troubles of these broken world. I didn't know at that time that I could always trust in the

Lord to be my strength. I had a broken spirit at the time and didn't feel the presence of God with me so I started to fall into a great darkness. I finally felt the experience of what it was like at that time to have a dad, other than the love that me and my grandfather shared. The love between Mark and us kids only lasted for a short period of time. After arriving at the funeral home Adam and I were browsing around looking at all the people that came to his funeral. This was the first time me, Adam and Ruth had ever been to a funeral. We were too young to understand what was going on. Especially Ruth, she was only a baby when Mark died. We were at the opening of the wake. A wake is when they have a showing of the body of the deceased. My grandpa took me and Adam up by the casket to see Mark while Ruth stayed with my mother Mary Kay. My grandpa had to lift me up to see Mark's body. Then when I seen Marks body I remember leaning over and reaching out my hand toward Mark with tears running down my face yelling "daddy, daddy wake up daddy please wake up and come home." as I grabbed his

cold hand while hoping he'd wake up out of his
peaceful slumber. Adam reached towards Mark and
gave him a kiss saying we love you daddy Mark as
tears were also running down his face too. I too also
gave Mark a kiss then we were told to say our final
goodbyes, but I was so angry and upset with tears
pouring down my face I did not want to say goodbye
in my mind I just wanted my daddy Mark back.
Grandpa had to take us to the back where the other
kids were, since I couldn't stop screaming and
crying. This was not an easy situation for Adam and
I. Grandpa Clay took us to his house for a few
weeks till my mom got things together. As the
funeral ended the next day; which was the burial of
Mark, and as they laid his body down into the
ground the minister had recited these words from

*(Ecclesiastes 12:7) "Then shall the dust return to the
earth as it was: and the spirit shall return unto God who
gave it."*

I was too young and depressed to realize what
that scripture meant. Soon after the funeral my mom
had to pack things up at the house as we could no

longer afford to live there on just my mothers income. Lynn chose to stay with her grandma, her real mom's mother for a while. Lynn still came to visit us from time to time and spent the nights at our place. She felt close to us and still considered us to be her family and we considered her to be part of our family as well even though she was in actual half/blood relation to Ruth she was still our sister. Still living on the westside of Cleveland, we found an apartment on Lorain Avenue where our mother was now a single mother again raising 3 kids on her own. My mom was very depressed and stressed after Mark's funeral. She had problems controlling her temper. She started taking a lot of her anger out on me and Adam. When Adam and I didn't clean our room our mother would get furious and start screaming and throwing things at us out of anger and rage. Adam and I got punished a lot with the belt and other things. My mom even grabbed me by the hair a few times. This was happening more often then usual. I felt scared and alone. I always called my grandpa and he'd know what to say to get me to calm down. My mom got mad at me when I called grandpa Clay. Grandpa would be so mad at her for the way she started treating Adam and I. Soon I began to feel a bitterness and anger toward our mother.

(Ephesians 4:31) says "Let all bitterness, and wrath, and anger, and clamour, and evil speaking, be put away from you, with all malice."

According to this scripture we were asked to let go of all bitterness and anger but I just didn't know how to let that go at the time. At this point in my life all I wanted was my grandpa Clay. I started to become more and more afraid of my mother and would hide in my closet a lot when I heard her screaming at Adam. I felt scared for my brother at times. Lynn even stopped coming around for a while since things were getting out of control. Sometimes when my mom went too far grandpa would come by the apartment to get her to calm down. They got into face to face arguments a lot. Then one day he suggested we all needed some type of grieving counseling seeing as we still didn't quite get over

Mark being gone and all. Mother had refused to believe she was still grieving. She did think it was a good idea to put Adam and I through grieving counseling. Our mother was still in that stage of denial. Feelings of denial can last for days, months, and sometimes years after the funeral service. One of the ways some people react to the pain of losing a loved one is to avoid thinking about it altogether. There are 5 stages of grief: 1 being in denial, 2 anger, 3 bargaining, 4 depression, and 5 acceptance. The bible teaches us in

(Luke 9:23) Jesus says "If anyone would come after me, let him deny himself and take up his cross daily and follow me. For whoever wants to save their life will lose it, but whoever loses their life for me will find it."

What does it mean to take up your cross? It simply means to turn our weaknesses into our greatest strengths as Jesus did when he died and suffered to free us from our sinful lives. So for the next 3 months we did counseling. They helped us cope with Mark's death in various different ways. We did some forms of different arts and crafts. We

decorated boxes as they told us to pick out some
things that once belonged to Mark, to put inside the
box as a keepsake. We met with grieving counselors
on a weekly basis. We did puzzles and games.
Mother's way of coping was having her guy friends
over for a few drinks and fun. The bible teaches us
this in:

(Proverbs 3:5) "Trust in the Lord with all your heart and
lean not on your own understanding."

What this means is to believe and trust in the Lord
and lean on him when we don't know which
direction to go or when times get hard in our life.
When we trust in the Lord with all our heart we
leave no room for doubt. Soon after a while my
mom stopped the harsh punishments for now. It was
now springtime, in the year of 1998. We were on
spring break from school. I was now 8 years old and
Adam was 11. Adam and I made some new friends
on the block. One day I was getting ready to play
outside when I walked past Ruth's room. I then
heard Ruth playing and making conversations with
someone. I noticed mother was downstairs in the

kitchen smoking a cigarette while talking on the phone. Adam was already outside waiting for me. Ruth was about 4 years old now. As I walked slowly up to the door, I cracked it open just a little and saw Ruth standing by the window while playing with her dolls. She was having a conversation with no one it seemed. I then walked in and asked Ruth who she was talking to. She then responded to me looking at me with a smile "I'm talking to daddy I'm showing him all my dolly's." I just shook my head in confusion and walked away meeting Adam outside as mother was coming upstairs to check on Ruth discovering the same thing I just witnessed.

(Revelation 21:4) "He will wipe away every tear from their eyes, and death shall be no more, neither shall there be mourning, nor crying, nor pain anymore, for the former things have passed away."

Ruth had been grieving in ways we did not understand. We all cried prayers through our tears. Jesus hears the cries of the little ones and answers. He lets us know in dreams and visions that our loved ones are ok and that through Him they are at peace.

God knows we're meant to experience grief in our lives, but were not meant to go through it alone. He wants us to seek comfort in Him. Relying on God can relieve sorrow to give that comfort and support we all so need. I then met up with Adam outside. There was a playground across the street that we spent a lot of time hanging out at with our new friends. I hung out with a girl named Kesha Thompson and her sister Alicia Thompson. We went to the playground a lot as kids because it was right across the street from the apartment complex where we were living at the time. The park was by nearby train tracks and there were woods that me and my friends used to play in. There was a time when we went on the train tracks just to explore. One day we were exploring the woods and came across what appeared to be a deep hole that looked like it was dug up, but no shovel was found. Upon discovering this hole we also found articles of clothing scattered throughout the woods. We then started to get a little curious and stared closely at the hole. Kesha decided to do some digging around but what she saw around the hole had her running out of the woods in fear. The hole seemed big enough to fit a really big sized dog. Then I began to see what Kesha was looking at and told Alicia who was still in the woods with me that it looked like two tips of someone's fingers but couldn't really tell because it was covered in dirt. After discovering that, Alicia and I took off as well in fear. At the time we were too confused with our imagination to what we had witnessed that day. We were not even sure of what we had seen as we were too young to even understand what we had discovered or didn't discover in those woods that day. Till this day we just remained silent about what we saw in those woods. We soon forgot about it. We still hang out at the playground but, never again did we step foot in those woods by the train tracks. Life was very challenging for me when I was a kid. I struggled with a lot of different fears throughout my life and new fears always came my way.

(2 Timothy 1:7) "For God has not given us the spirit of fear, but of power and love, and of a sound mind."

The bible also teaches us that we can overcome our fears, doubts and mournings through Jesus Christ. In time Adam and I went back to school after 3 weeks of missing school due to Mark's death. We had a lot of catching up to do. So we spent the last 2 months of school getting all caught up before the summer, so we would be able to pass and move on to the next grade. Our mother got a job working at the grocery store being a cashier at Tops supermarket. She seemed happy again working and socializing with other people. It was now a year after Mark's death and our mom seemed to have moved on with her life or so we thought. I was still sad in some ways with the loss of Mark. School and hanging out with friends put my mind at ease for the time being from sadness. Also visiting with grandpa Clay and grandma Asa really put things at an ease for me. After Mark's death we stopped going to church, it seemed that my mom just stopped caring and wanted to do her own things in life. We as kids were too young to care or understand God's plan for us in life.

(Isaiah 53:6) "We all, like sheep, have gone astray; Each of us has turned to his own way; and the Lord has laid on him the iniquity of us all."

Chapter 4
Spirits of Iniquity

It was the beginning of 1999. Our mom had introduced us to a guy she met at work named Gilbert Rogers. At first they were just friends but then it seemed to be more than that when they started kissing and holding hands. A few months passed by and my mom and Gilbert got married. My mother was now Mary Kay Rogers and was no longer a Saunders anymore. Soon after that Gilbert moved in with us. We then looked for a bigger place as our family was about to get bigger when mom was pregnant again with my new soon to be baby sister. I was so excited to be a big sister again. I couldn't wait to meet my new baby sister. We moved to a nicer area in Cleveland, a house with 4 bedrooms. Lynn even started coming back around more. She came back on halloween night drunk, asking my mom if she could move in. Mother let

her stay in the spare bedroom in the basement.
Meanwhile after Lynn got all settled in, my mom
enrolled us into a different school system.   We were
now in Old Brooklyn city schools. Elementary
school wasn't so bad till I got to middle school.
That's when things really got bad for me. It was the
year 2000 when I started middle school at Rhodes
middle school.   I was very quiet and hardly talked to
anybody. I was known as the weirdest kid in school.
I got picked on nearly every day and it wasn't just
name calling, things got physical too over the years.
I felt rage building up inside and I just wanted
revenge on everyone that hurt me in school.

*(Romans 12:19) "Dearly beloved, avenge not
yourselves, but rather give place unto wrath: for it is
written, Vengeance is mine; I will repay, saith the Lord."*

The Lord teaches us that revenge on others is never
the answer in solving our issues with our enemies
but to give all our troubles unto the Lord and he will
take care of our problems. Boys picked on me the
most because I looked like a boy with my hair so
short and ragged looking, sometimes I'd dress like a

boy wearing saggy old clothes that were a little too big on me, and I even had pimples on my face after starting puberty. The kids used to call me pizza face. I became the laughing stock in the whole school by 8th grade. I remember when the boys at school would spit on me and shove me into lockers. One time one boy almost pushed me off the auditorium stage. My ankle had a sprain from it. Even on my way home from school while walking home I got harassed and picked on some more. I walked home from school every day crying. Sometimes they were so cruel I just felt like I wanted to die asking God why this had to happen to me.

(Psalms 34:17) "The righteous cry out, and the Lord hears them, he delivers them from all their troubles."

We don't always understand what God has in mind for us or the plans he has for us. At this time I had no clue what God had in store for me. I cried a lot on my way home from school asking God why does this keep happening to me? Or why can't I make any friends and why are kids so cruel? God hears our cries and he knows our pain. I just needed to know him closer and learn to hear the sound of his voice calling out to me. I didn't understand how to listen to his voice or anyone for that matter. Things weren't going well at home either. My mom and I were not getting along. We got into physical arguments with each other. There was a lot of negative language between me and my mother. One time she even put me out of the house one day because I scratched her down alongside of her arm. Then she began bleeding. I didn't feel bad for what I did wrong at the time. I was angry and outraged and full of hate toward my mom. Then I was screaming and saying awful things to her as she was saying awful and cruel things back toward me. She really gave me a good whooping and locked me out until I cooled down my rage towards her. She threatened to call the cops on me a few times. At times I did to. At this time I was consumed with hatred towards her and the kids at school that were bullying me. I cried my self to sleep every night and even tried hurting myself a lot. I felt like I didn't know what else to do in that moment.

(Exodus 20:12) "Honor your father and mother, that your days may be long in the land that the Lord your God is giving you."

God teaches us in His Word that we are suppose honor our parents and respect them. I had no respect for my mother at this time. School was very rough for me. I got in trouble a lot for skipping classes so the teachers always gave me detention. I spent most of my time skipping classes in the girls bathroom hiding in a stall crying my eyes out because of all the hurt from other kids, mostly from the immature boys.

(Deuteronomy 31:6) "Be strong and courageous, Do not be afraid or terrified because of them, for the Lord your God goes with you; he will never leave you nor forsake you."

At this time in my life I did not feel the presence of the Lord, I felt like I was falling deeper and deeper into darkness. I came into the girls bathroom one day and found three girls sitting on the ground in a circle playing with stones and creepy looking symbols on the floor with candles all around. I didn't understand at the time what dark things we were getting ourselves into. I then realized they were dealing with some dark forces. I was interested in anything to take the pain away. The Lord says:

(Leviticus 19:26) "You shall not eat any flesh with the blood in it: You shall not interpret omens or tell fortunes."

Witchcraft is very demonic and of the devil and can bring curses unto yourself and your family. I didn't understand back then what witchcraft was. I met a boy named Jack who was into things like that, he was my first boyfriend. He was getting bullied too. I was only 13 and he was 14 years old and a grade ahead of me. I felt some sort of connection with him since we were both going through things at school and at home. Jack's mom left him and his dad when Jack was just a young boy. I went over to his house a few times and noticed a lot of satanic writings on his bedroom walls. He listened to a lot of dark heavy metal music. After a few months of hooking up with him I realized how mean and disrespectful he was to me. He was also the first boyfriend I had who hurt me by grabbing my arm while digging his nails into me. He hit me in the face a few times after a long argument. My mom didn't even notice the red marks on my face. I walked to my room in silence trying not to even think about.

> *(Proverbs 3:25-26) "Be not afraid of sudden terror, or the ruin of the wicked, when it comes, For the Lord will be your confidence, and will keep your foot from being caught."*

At this time I didn't have any confidence nor did I have much faith at this point. Then after a while Jack and I stopped talking. I never did tell my mom about the things Jack did and said to me. Things were getting worse at home. My mom got sick after she had my new baby sister Elizabeth Marie Rogers, but we just called her Lizzie for short. Adam and I helped mom out with taking care of Lizzie. I loved Lizzie and Ruth both even though I didn't show it that much. Our mother soon started having a lot of health issues. She was in and out of the hospital a lot so it was up to Adam and I to manage things around the house while taking care of Ruth and Lizzie. Mom started feeling depressed again since Gilbert was hardly ever home anymore. All he did was work all the time even though my mom needed him to take care of her while she was sick. A lot of anger and rage started stirring up in our home between my mom and I. We got into a lot of fist fights. There were times she had dragged me by the hair. I've scratched her a few times while throwing some punches after. She had me one time in a corner where she attacked me out of rage and hatred towards me and I fought back. In time I felt bad for a lot of the things I had done to my mother. I was just consumed with anger and filled with a lot of mixed emotions. My mom slept a lot and didn't seem to get out much because of her sickness. She blamed Adam and I a lot for her sickness and depression. We still continued to fight and argue almost on a daily basis.

(Proverbs 17:22) "A joyful heart is good medicine: but a crushed spirit dries up the bones."

I really couldn't stand being around my mom at this time. I hated her and she hated me. Hate is a strong word according to what the bible teaches us.

(Proverbs 10:12) "Hatred stirs up strife, but love covers all offenses."

In time I needed to learn to let go of my anger and hatred towards not only my mom but to everyone else that has done me wrong. Our physical fights continued on. My mom put me in the hospital once or twice. We had social services threatening to take us away from our home. I was scared of my mom for a while because of all the violence and screaming in the house. I was also afraid of social services taking me and my siblings away. Deep down I loved my siblings and didn't want us to be apart. It was bad enough I had separation anxiety from not always being around my grandfather; but the thought of never seeing him or my siblings again was really scaring me to death. I tried hanging myself a few times in the basement but I only just passed out.

(1 John 4:18) "There is no fear in love, but perfect love drives out fear, because fear has to do with punishment, the one who fears is not made perfect in love."

I really did have a hard time with love because I hated my mom. The kids at school made my life hard with all the bullying. I had no love for myself because of my insecurity. Jesus says in bible:

(Matthew 6:15) "But if you do not forgive others their trespasses, neither will your Father forgive your trespasses."

It took me a very long time to learn forgiveness. At this time I was not ready or willing to forgive and let go. I was still holding on to a lot of anger and hatred, that in time I would have to learn to let go and give it to God in heaven. My mom took up babysitting a lot for the neighbors since she couldn't work because of her sickness. This was her type of work to make money I guess you could say. I also used to take my sister's and their friends to the park to play just to get out of the house and away from my mom. We all made friends with a neighbor

down the street from 2 blocks down. Her name was
Juanita Fontez. Then one day I was taking a walk
down the street to meet up with Juanita and my sister
Ruth. Ruth had just spent the night over Juanita's.
We were getting ready to meet up at the park when a
neighbor from 4 houses down stopped me and asked
me if I could help him with some yard work for his
grandma. I knew his grandma but didn't know she
had a grandson. She was a friendly old lady. I had a
paper route and always delivered newspapers to her
while she sat on her porch patiently waiting for her
newspaper, always smiling and saying hello to me. I
wondered where that sweet old lady was. He
explained she had to go to the store and was going to
be back later. He also explained to me that he was
helping his grandma with the yard that afternoon.
Her grandson seemed nice and friendly so I decided
to help him. After talking to him while working in
the backyard in the hot sun, I realized he knew a lot
of people from the neighborhood and was best
friends with Juanita's older brother Alejandro
Fontez. He then offered me to come inside for

something cold to drink since it was the middle of summer and it was hot. I felt uncomfortable at first about going inside his Grandma's house since I really didn't know him that well. I was very thirsty and really wanted something cold to drink so he insisted. He took me inside then poured me a drink and gave it to me. He then started staring at me while putting his fingers through my hair. This wasn't at all as I suspected it to be and I started feeling very uncomfortable being around him. After I drank my cold drink and put down my cup he then started touching me in inappropriate places that I was too young to even understand. I was still only around 13 at the time this happened and this guy was around 19. He then took me by the hand and guided me towards the basement where he slowly started to take off his clothes till he was completely naked. I was so speechless and afraid and didn't know how to comprehend all of this. I just submitted in fear to everything he told me to do. He then guided his hand along with mine to his front private area. He made me begin to pleasure himself until the act of evil ended then sent me on out the door. I just walked straight home after that with tears falling down my face. I was filled with such shame and sadness and confusion. I felt so scared and too afraid to even say a word to anyone about what had happened. Adam went to get Ruth from Juanita's since I had disappeared for so long. After that day I stayed home grounded to my room for a while lying in bed speechless not knowing how to wrap my head around what happened and why it happened?   I was even too afraid and still confused about the incident to tell my mom. She was already mad that Adam had to go get Ruth from her friends house while wondering where I was. I was too afraid that if I told her what happened she would not believe me. I didn't know what to expect if I told her, so I just stayed silent about the whole thing.   The bible explains to those with a fearful heart:

(Isaiah 35:4) "Be strong, do not fear; your God will come, he will come with vengeance; with divine retribution he will come to save you."

I wanted so much to become strong but my spirit was just too weak. In the summer of 2004 I was 14 years old. My mom had just got acquainted with the lady Rosia Hernandez and her two kids down the street. They were very new to Cleveland Ohio. They were from Queens, New York. Her oldest was her daughter Marie Hernandez and her youngest was her son Antonio Hernandez. Antonio was around the same age as me and Marie was 17. Antonio and I became friends. I thought he was cute at the time and liked him, but I didn't think he liked me. Eventually we got to holding hands then called each other boyfriend and girlfriend. I was very shy and had self doubts about myself. I guess you can say it was a summer fling. Things were going good at first but then he came on strong with his kisses and what I mean by strong, I mean he was very rough. He would grab my face very rough-like while he was squeezing my cheeks together with full force when he'd kiss me. He bit me a lot on the neck and I didn't like it. Antonio had a lot of anger problems. Sometimes we got into these minor disagreements.

He'd take it out on me with physical behavior. Behaviors can be caused by the behaviors of a parent or the absence of a parent. Antonio's sister said their dad was very abusive towards them. Their mom divorced and left Queens to get away from their dad. Antonio also got physical with me a lot. Sometimes Lynn would help cover up some of the bruises with her make up, so mother didn't grow suspicious of what was going on. We were both too afraid of what my mom would say or think. Then one day my mom left to go to the store with Lynn. My sister and her friend Juanita played outside in the backyard. Antonio demanded for me to meet him in the basement. So I met him in the basement and then he told me to follow him to the back room of the basement were the spare room was. Then he started putting his hands on me with physical force. I was still a virgin at 14 years old. I was confused and too scared and nervous to understand what was going on in this situation. He then grabbed me with full force as I was making my way to hurry to the door while planning to escape. He then pulled me by the arm and told me to get on the ground. I then started to become very nervous and scared. He told me to lay down on the ground and not to make a sound or any sudden movement or he'll hurt me again. At that moment I just wanted to scream and cry but I was too afraid of what he would do to me if I did that. He then began touching me inappropriately all over my body hushing me to not say a word. I kept telling him to please stop but he would just keep going. This is when I really began to feel more and more uncomfortable and frightened. I started fidgeting around and saying stop repeatedly. Then he'd get angry and restrain my arms while covering my mouth with his hands. His pants came down and that's when he started to do the unspeakable act of evil unto me. I yelled stop so many times out of fear with my heart pounding rapidly and tears of worry falling down the side of my face in that moment I just felt like wanting my life to end. I just couldn't take the pain and hurt anymore. He just kept putting his hand over my mouth while throwing a few punches at me to keep me silenced. Then soon after

the evil act started it suddenly stopped. My sister
Ruth and Juanita had flown open the door to ask
what was going on. They didn't hear the screams
but came into the house to see where I had
disappeared to. Antonio quickly jumped right off
me as they came in while covering up his pride.
Antonio had lied to them and said we were just
playing a game, but we know that's not the truth at
all. My sister and her friend knew and saw the fear
in my eyes as I stood there speechless ready to ball
my eyes out but forcing myself to hold back my
tears as I wanted to be strong when really I was very
weak. I then dashed out of the room in fear. I said
to myself to never talk about what just happened at
this point in my life ever again. I felt very insecure
about myself shortly after that. It was bad enough I
had already felt some way about my looks because
of all the kids that made fun of me in junior high.
Antonio and I stopped talking after that, and
eventually broke up. I felt like I hated him after that.
I had mixed emotions about what he did to me in
that dark basement. I felt so low and insecure about

myself after the whole incident. There are many different levels of insecurity, but among them is the lack of trust and confidence in God. God has given us the purpose for our lives, the purpose to remove all doubt we have, that's part of his plan for us. Doubting is the work of satan.

(Ephesians 6:12) "For we wrestle not against flesh and blood, but against principalities, against powers, against rulers of the darkness of this world, against spiritual wickedness in high places."

I was definitely wrestling with a darkness inside of me that was torturing my mind for a long time. Things at home with my family weren't getting any easier for me either. My step dad Gilbert was working a lot and over the years he was working 2 jobs. He was barely ever home. When he was home all his attention and focus was on Lizzie. He didn't pay too much attention to me or Adam. I was consumed by hate and jealousy. He talked to Ruth a little bit only because Ruth and Lizzie had gotten really close. Sometimes I take a drive with him to the Eastside of Cleveland, since that's where he worked. I only rode with him to work sometimes because grandpa Clay would pick me up at Gilbert's work place every time I stayed the weekend at grandpa's house. Car rides on the way to Gilbert's work were always silent. I always just stared out the window and he'd focus on driving with nothing to say. If it wasn't for my mom asking to take me with him so grandpa Clay could pick me up at his work, Gilbert would not have done it. It was hard feeling rejected by Gilbert, whom we started calling dad. He didn't seem like a dad, nor did I feel like he even cared about us like Mark did. I still mourned over the loss of Mark from time to time wishing he was still here with us. One night I had a dream about Mark but it didn't seem like a normal dream. It felt so real! I saw this place surrounded by bright light. There was Mark standing there by what appeared to be a doorway in a room looking straight at me with a comforting smile. I felt a sense of peace and didn't want to ever wake up from this dream. I missed him so much just wanting him to come home and be my dad again.

(John 14:1-3) "Let not your hearts be troubled. Believe in God; believe also in me. In my Father's house there are many rooms. If it were not so, would I have told you that I would go and prepare a place for you? And if I go and prepare a place for you, I will come again and take you to myself, that where I am you may be also."

God wants us to trust him even through our mournings and sufferings. I believe the Lord had brought me comfort in that dream. Comfort that I didn't understand just yet. I was still in a battle of my own thoughts and feelings that I didn't know what to make of it. In that moment I finally felt a sense that Mark was in a place somewhere better than this world. As the months went by I tried to get along with the kids in the neighborhood. I felt fearful and emotionally hurt by people to make friends with anyone. Ruth became best friends with Juanita. They were around the same age and liked to do a lot of fun activities together. At this time in my story is when I really felt depressed and unloved. I felt like Ruth and I drifted apart. I was so happy to be a big sister to both Ruth and Lizzie. Then I felt as if I failed at that and just about everything at that point in my life too. Adam was almost 18 and ready to move out which made me even more depressed. Adam and I were very close. When he was hanging out with his friends he would be acting some type of way toward me. He was very mean to me when he was around his friends. He started working with Gilbert after he turned 17 at the factory that Gilbert worked at. Lynn had gotten pregnant after her trip from Florida. My mom picked her up from the greyhound station. She soon gave birth to her son Cory, then left shortly after to never return. My mom then took Cory in as her own son. Lynn had just left Cory in the arms of our care. We all accepted him as our youngest sibling after Lizzie. I now had a younger brother. With Adam being gone all the time with his friends, Ruth and I helped mom out with Lizzie and Cory. Things just only got worse and I felt resentment with my siblings. Ruth seemed aggravated with me and Lizzie was a tattle tale. Always telling our mother what I'm doing or what I'm not doing. Then I would get back handed in the mouth for saying the wrong thing to Lizzie. Gilbert attacked me once for not listening to my mom and being mean to my sisters. Cory was just a baby at the time and mom wanted me to help her watch him all the time while she slept or went to the store. Things were starting to really fall apart at home. I felt no love in the house or anywhere. I made my room in the basement away from all my siblings. I felt no connection with them any more. The only person I wanted to be around was my grandpa Clay. I would cry myself to sleep almost every night praying and asking God in my own way if he would just take the pain I felt in my heart far from me. I felt like I sunk into a dark valley of depression. I felt totally and completely alone, like nobody cares, and no one is listening. I felt isolated, cut off, and in my heart at that time I felt like everyone abandoned me, But Jesus said:

(Matthew 11:28) "Come to me, all who labor and are heavy laden, and I will give you rest."

Jesus gives rest for us that are weary and troubled. As I got older into my teenage years things really took a turn for the worst and there was no rest for me at this point.

Chapter 5
Rest For The Weak In Spirit

By fall of 2004 we finally decided to go back to church as a family. My sister's friend from school Shelly introduced us to a church her and her family were going to. The name of the church was Oak View Bible church. It was a nice size christian church. When we went to the sanctuary we saw where the pastor preached. There on the wall was a scripture and it said:

(John 14:6) Jesus said to them,"I am the way, and the truth, and the life. No one comes to the father except through me."

I didn't quite understand what that meant yet, but I knew in time I would find out. We eventually started going on a weekly basis. Our mom signed all of us up for the Awana's club.   At Awana's we recited our pledge of allegiance to the american flag, the Awana flag and the bible. They always pick people to hold the flags and the bible. We had to memorize these pledges. One night our youth leader asked me to hold the bible and we recited "I pledge allegiance to the bible God's holy word, I will make it a lamp unto my feet, and a light unto my path. I will hide his words in my heart so that I might not sin against God." Then the church shouted "Amen!" Awana's is a Wednesday night youth club where we have fun playing games and memorizing verses and winning awards and prizes for completing our bible verse booklet. One verse in particular that I remember:

> (Romans 6:23) "For the wages of sin is death, but the gift of God is eternal life through Christ Jesus our Lord."

So what this verse means is that when you receive something good which is the gift that God has to offer. That something happens to you that changes your life in such a way, even though we may not deserve this wonderful gift God offers unto us, he still loves us enough to offer his son Jesus to change our lives and make us new and whole in Him when we believe. In time we also went on spiritual retreats. We did a lot of activities when we went on our retreats. We stayed in cabins and went hiking while learning about the things God created. We had a lot fun going camping with the church. Those were annual yearly events. In the summertime me and my family always helped with the camps and volunteered at vacation bible school. We also did fun things around the fall like trunk or treat or even the harvest ball where we got to dress up in our favorite costumes and win prizes. Winter was fun too. We went to some of the senior citizens homes and sang Christmas carols and helped out with Operation christmas child. Which is helping families that are in need of help around the holidays. In the year of 2004, spring was just around the corner. In early March the church planned a special event for the youth group. It was a fun experience at Acquire the Fire concert in downtown Cleveland at the Wolstein center. We met at the church late that evening and rode in the company van to Acquire the Fire. When finally we arrived at the christian concert and I was just so amazed. I thought to myself I had never been to a christian concert or any concert. This was my first experience I will never forget. Our youth pastor gave us our tickets to our seats. So me and my brother Adam and his new girlfriend Laura sat together. We all sat close together. Our youth group filled two rows in one section. This was the beginning of a great and powerful new experience for me.

(2 Thessalonians 2:14) "To this he called you through our gospel, so that you may obtain the glory of our Lord Jesus Christ."

As the bands started playing their christian gospel music I looked around and saw people lifting up their hands to the sky. I didn't understand what they were doing because our church was old fashioned and did not do things like that. The music they played was so powerful, touching and heartwarming. I started feeling like I had goosebumps all over my body. I didn't realize that it was the power of the Holy Spirit at the time. Then I heard this song play that really touched my heart in such a way I couldn't quite comprehend. The name of the song was

"Here I am to worship" by Hillsong. It was such a beautiful song that I have never heard before and will never forget. As the song played a guy was talking on the stage and he said if anyone has never received Jesus as their Lord and savior to come forward now. Then suddenly, I felt this urge in my spirit to come down by the stage to talk to someone. I've never felt this way before it appeared to be a feeling I didn't quite understand. I felt God lifting me up that day. I was new to this strange feel. I felt my heart crying out to Jesus, asking that he would ment my broken heart to put it back together.

(Psalms 147:3) "He heals the brokenhearted and binds up their wounds."

God can repair the wounds of people's crushed hearts. There were a few people who also took that step in coming down to meet with someone to pray with including my brother Adam. I remember meeting with some of these people who were ministers and took us backstage and started praying with us individually. I had no idea what I was doing but in my heart God knew this was where he wanted me to be. The Lord was stretching out his hand pulling me closer to him. The person that met with me took my hands and said bow your head and repeat these words unto God from the bottom of your heart. He said as I repeated, "Heavenly father we come to you right now because I have Grace Lockwood here and she wants to surrender her life unto you through your son Jesus Christ. Jesus I surrender my life to you. It is yours forever please forgive me of all my sins. I believe you died and rose again, and that you are my Lord and savior forever and ever Amen." As I was done praying, I was given a hug and headed back towards my seat. I felt tears I had never felt before running down my face. They were not sad tears or crying from hurt and pain type of tears. They were joyful tears!

(Galatians 2:20) "I have been crucified with Christ, it is no longer I who live, but Christ who lives in me, And the life I now live in the flesh I live by faith in the Son of God, who loved me and gave himself for me."

In that moment I felt a chill going up and down my spine with tears of joy just pouring down my face.

This was indeed the Spirit of God beginning to work in my life with a new chapter. When everyone who had come forward with me was done praying, the last band came on which was the famous christian rock band Skillet. It was the first time I had ever heard that kind of music and I liked it. After that the concert had ended and we all got back in the van and headed back to church to meet up with our families to pick us up. That was one of the best nights of my life. One that I will never forget. When we had church that following Sunday they announced my upcoming baptism since I became born again.

(John 3:3) Jesus answered him, "Truly, truly, I say to you, unless one is born again he cannot see the kingdom of God." This was still new to me so I was still in the process of understanding what this all meant. The bible makes it clear about the concept of being born again. The bible clearly says:

(John 3:6) "That which is born of the flesh is flesh, and that which is born of the Spirit is spirit."

Only by accepting the truth in your heart that Jesus is Lord, and believing that he gave his life as a ransom for you makes you born again in the spirit.

(Romans 3:23) "For all have sinned and fall short of the glory of God."

We all want peace, love and a sound mind in our life but it's only through Jesus that we can have these things. As my story continues I did end up getting baptized in Pastor Samual's swimming pool. That was my pastor of Oak View bible church where I went. I grew up having a lot of memories of that church, but my story doesn't stop here.

(1 Peter 5:8) "Be alert and of sober mind, your enemy the devil prowls around like a roaring lion looking for someone to devour."

Indeed the enemy was not done with me yet and my faith was weak at this point, so I was still an easy target for the devil to devour.

Chapter 6
The Spirit of The Hungry Lion

Even though I had just gave my life to Christ I was not truly walking with him in the spirit. Jesus says:

(John 6:63) "It is the Spirit who gives life; the flesh profits nothing; the words that I have spoken to you are spirit and are life."

I was new to the faith and not yet understanding it either. I was not ready to fully commit to the faith. The year of 2004 was the year I started my freshmen year at Brooklyn high school. I ran track and field at the start of my first year of high school. I felt at ease when I ran track. I also started to make friends. High school was also the mother load of lustful desires and temptation. Temptation is all around us even when we don't see it. The desire to do something wrong and unwise is also known as temptation. Even Jesus himself was tempted by the devil.

(Matthew 4:7) Jesus said unto him, "It is written again, thou shalt not tempt the Lord thy God."

Temptation was a big struggle for me in high school because I was interested in so many things. Boys for one thing, and popularity was a big interest that I had. I also experienced a lot of lustful desires in many various ways. Because of all the things that had happened to me in the past I had curious desires for the same sex.

(Leviticus 18:22) "You shall not lie with a male as with a woman; it is an abomination to the Lord."

This verse makes the bible clear that God disapproves of sex between the same sex. Jesus makes it clear that marrige is between man and woman.

(Matthew 19:4) He answered, "Have you not read that he who created them from the beginning made them male and female."

My friend Anna from elementary school went to the same high school as me. I found out she was bisexual and secretly had a crush on me. Which meant she was interested in sexual immorality and fornications which according to the bible is a sin. I didn't know at the time that what I was doing was wrong and against God's laws. I did partake in some sexual immoral behavior with Anna.

(1 Corinthians 6:18) "Flee from sexual immorality; every other sin a person commits is outside the body, but the sexually immoral person sins against his own body."

Sexual immorality is someone who participates in adultery, fornication, hemosexual and lesbian behavior or any other unholy or unnatural and impure sexual activity. At this time most of my interest was in boys. From the trauma and pain I went through with boys, I became so confused and traumatized that I was willing to try something different just to fit in. I was making friends for all the wrong reasons. I continued to participate in some sexually immoral behavior between Anna and I, looking for attention not realizing the consequences of my wrongdoing. In my heart it felt wrong, but my mind was telling me yes just go for it. Which was the temptations and voices of the evil one.

(Matthew 6:13) "And lead us not into temptation but, deliver us from the evil one. For Yours is the kingdom, and the power, and the glory forever. Amen."

Lord knows at this point I needed to be delivered but was not ready for deliverance just yet. Soon it was fall of 2004, and I went to my first homecoming dance. A guy named Ryan asked me out to homecoming. I was so excited no guy has ever asked me out before like that. He played on the basketball team so that was a plus in my mind for popularity. I actually started having more friends in high school than I did in junior high. I thought to myself high school is going to be great, but little did I know, I was heading down a dark and dangerous path. I was always nervous around the boys because I never felt loved or ever really felt attractive. At least in my mind that's how I always felt. I was so consumed by jealousy and envious of other girls.

(Proverbs 27:4) "Anger is cruel, and wrath is like a flood, but jealousy is even more dangerous."

I was very self conscious of myself about things that had happened to me in the past. So talking to boys wasn't easy for me. I struggled to make new friends, but when other kids talked to me first I began to open up more. Homecoming was a lot of fun. I got to dance with Ryan and we even started dating. We held hands and kissed from time to time. I thought wow I finally have my happily ever after until two months later Ryan broke up with me and left me for another girl. I felt so heart broken for the first time in a while. I thought I was in love but I was so wrong. I went to the gym that day and just sat on the steps near the track when nobody was around and just swam in a river of my tears thinking no boys will ever like me. I felt like such a freak.

(1 Corinthians 10:13) "No temptation has overtaken you except what is common to mankind, And God is faithful; he will not let you be tempted beyond what you can bear, but

when you are tempted, he will also provide a way out so that you can endure it."

I thought to myself many times that there was no hope for me. Months went by and my jealousy became anger and rage. One day I got into a physical fight at school with a boy named DJ because he started messing with me. I started filling up with so much rage and hatred. I then forcefully pushed him then shoved him into the lockers. I cursed and swore at him. He pushed back but I wasn't ready to give up a fight. After that the teachers had made sure he kept his distance from me and I too had to keep my distance. We both got detention after school.

(Colossians 3:8) "But now you must put them all away: anger, wrath, malice, slander, and obscene talk from your mouth."

After a while I just kept my distance from people to avoid conflict. In spring of 2005 I met a boy named Brandon. He was quiet and quite shy. He was close friends with my brother Adam. They hung out a lot and were both seniors in high school. My brother was dating Brandon's step sister Analynn. Adam was taking her to prom. My brother Adam suggested to Brandon that he should take me to the prom. Brandon had agreed with Adam. I was flattered with excitement. Brandon and I started dating. We became boyfriend and girlfriend before the week of prom. My brother Adam also received his first car as a graduation gift donated by our church family. Many of the members donated the funds toward the vehicle. It was an old gray 1990's Cadillac Allante. My brother Adam drove us all to prom in his new car. Prom was the night that really changed my thought process to wander off asstray, like a stray dog lost from his home. After the prom dance, we went to an after prom party at Brandon's house. I had my first sip of alcohol and it was the first night I willingly lost my virginity. The night amazed me. I never felt so wanted before and I loved the feeling of being wanted.

(1 John 1:9) "If we confess our sins, he is faithful and just to forgive us our sins and to cleanse us from all unrighteousness."

Brandon wasn't exactly the romantic type but he seemed to be the only boy that didn't hurt me. He used to surprise me at my locker just to talk to me and give me hugs and kisses. I felt a sense of being happy for the first time in my lonely life. Brandon, my brother Adam, and Analynn all graduated in 2005. After Adam's Graduation he moved out and had got a place of his own. Fall of 2005 I started my sophomore year in high school. Brandon and I were still together. Brandon got me my first job at dominos pizza working under the table. Brandon delivered pizza. His parents bought him a used car to get him back and forth to work to deliver pizzas. He'd pick me up after school to take me to work. We worked the same hours at dominos. His friend TJ even worked there too. TJ didn't like the boss man that we worked for at dominos pizza. His name was Yosef. He was from the country Libya. TJ quit one night after him and Yosef got into an argument.

Then TJ spit on the window of the Dominos shop and yelled out some swear words. TJ got so angry at Yosef. While Brandon was making deliveries, I stayed inside the store and was taught to make pizzas. The Boss man came up from behind me and began to grop his hands all over me, touching me in places that made me feel uncomfortable. I didn't know much about the boss man Yosef. He was an older man and made me feel uncomfortable all the time. Sometimes when Brandon would get back from delivering pizzas Yosef wanted to see us in his office. He paid us in cash at the end of the night but before that he always made an offer for us to make more money. He told Brandon and I to do things we didn't feel comfortable doing with each other while he watched and pleasured himself. We needed the money so we pursued what he had asked. I felt confused and disgusted with myself. I see why TJ didn't like him. The man had such a perverted mind. I was there for only a few months. Then I quit working there soon before the holidays came around. I skipped school sometimes to go over Brandon's place when his parents were at work. We smoked and drank a lot. I didn't care much about school. I just cared to be close to Brandon all the time. Without being around Brandon I would feel alone in my mind. I was very depressed and felt alone all the time. In the book of Psalms David says:

(Psalms 25:16-17) "Turn to me and be gracious to me, for I am lonely and afflicted. Relieve the troubles of my heart and free me from my anguish."

David needed the Lord's friendship because he felt lonely and distressed. Loneliness is common, but it can be very distressing, especially if circumstances are harsh. Regardless of how distressing circumstances are for God's people, the Lord will never forsake us. He is with us always no matter what situations we are in or the circumstances. God was always with me as my friend even when I didn't see it or feel it. In reality I was never alone as I thought I was. One night Brandon's mom and step dad got into a fight and his step dad kicked him out. My mom said it was ok that he lived with us for a while. My mom and I were still at it with our fights and arguments. With Brandon now living with us he tried stepping in between our fights, angering my mom's temper. With Adam not being around anymore I felt a sense of security when I was around Brandon. He soon began accompanying me to some of the church events we had around the holidays. We did hay riding in the fall and had Christmas eve service following Christmas caroling after that. He even came with me sometimes to church on Sundays.   It was nice having Brandon stay with us while it lasted. Eventually his mom divorced his step dad and got her and Brandon a new apartment. He then moved out into the new apartment with his mom. He still came to see me before and after school everyday. I felt worried at first when he moved out. soon began skipping school more to go see him. I then continued smoking cigarettes and trying drugs for the first time. Brandon and I were together almost every day. We felt so happy together or so I thought till I met Trinity. Trinity was a popular girl on the cheerleading squad. She was highly conceited of herself and was also full of drama. I skipped school a lot to hangout with Trinity. Trinity and I were very close at the time and did everything together. She got me into taking some hard drugs. She even sneaked me into bars with a fake ID she gave me. I was almost 16 when I met Trinity. We shared the same medical condition. Doctor Sue Jackson introduced me to Trinity when we rode together to the same camp recommended by doctor Sue. Trinity also looked like a model. I felt very envious of her.

(Proverbs 14:30) "A heart at peace gives life to the body, but envy rots the bones."

Envy comes from the lack of belief that God is all powerful, and cares about you deeply and has wonderful plans for your life.

(Psalm 37:1-2) "Do not fret because of those who are evil, or be envious of those who do wrong; for like the grass they will soon wither, like green plants they will soon die away."

Trinity was the start of what is called peer pressure but through the christian faith it is called demonic influence.   What is demonic influence exactly, well demonic influence can attack the body, mind, and soul. An evil spirit can attach themselves to someone who is very broken in spirit and can cause that person to live in an oppressed lifestyle. Being oppressed can cause mental illness by demonic spirits. The evil spirit can then dominate the mind of that oppressed person and then can spiritually attack another person.

(John 10:10) "The thief does not come except to steal, and to kill, and to destroy; I have come that they may have life, and that they may have it more abundantly."

Jesus came into the world so we can experience a life of prosperity and be filled with a joyful life through the Holy Spirit. Evil spirits will try and attempt to steal a person's soul by destroying the mind, body, and spirit of that person. For example when we hear these whispers telling us in our mind "hey its ok to try something new what harm can it do." That is the enemy the devil giving you those ideas which is also temptation.   Soon a person may be consumed by these evil spirits of infirmity the more they give in to the temptations of these evil spirits. Only then will they be further away from the love of God that is in Jesus Christ our Lord.

(2 Timothy 4:3-4) "For the time is coming when people will not endure sound teaching, but having itching ears they will accumulate for themselves teachers to suit their own passions, and will turn away from listening to the truth and wander off into myths."

I had no idea what I was getting myself into when I met Trinity. I liked the temptations and found myself drowning in my lustful desires. After a few years of dating Brandon and broke up. I found out he was secretly into Trinity and very attracted to her. That made me so jealous. Rumors were going around school. People were saying that Brandon was trying to sleep with her behind my back. I was so upset about people talking and saying these things. When I confronted Brandon he pretended he had no idea what everybody was talking about. I felt like he was lying. I soon ended our relationship. Trinity always played the victim in everything. She acted like she had no idea what was going on. Trinity secretly invited Brandon over to one of her party's while I was still in school. Her and Brandon got drunk together and that's when he tried making his move on Trinity. The truth is she wanted attention by making herself look innocent while she manipulated everyone. The definition for manipulation is to control or influence a person or situation cleverly, unfairly, or unscrupulously.

(2 Corinthians 11:14) "And no wonder, for even Satan disguises himself as an angel of light." (Galatians 6:7) "Do not be deceived: God is not mocked, for whatever one sows, that will he also reap."

What is manipulation again? Manipulation is also a form of emotional abuse influenced and brought on by demonic spirits. By this time I was so manipulated by Trinity she practically had me right where she wanted me all wrapped around her finger.

Chapter 7
The Power Of The Controlling Spirit

In 2006 I landed a job at Wendy's. I always used to walk to and from school and work. It seemed more convenient for me at the time plus I was physically active. Throughout my years of high school I continued to run track and field. Summer of 2006 I got my first car. My mom had given me her old beat up blue Ford. I didn't care, I liked it and it got me to and from work and school. Fall of 2006 school started back up again and it was my junior year of high school. I got into my first car accident and injured 4 other people that were in my car. The car was a total wreck. Thankfully everyone was alright with a few minor cuts and bruises. I was sent to the hospital by ambulance. I stayed at the hospital overnight because I was in critical condition. The doctors said I had a concussion. The seatbelt cut my throat open a little bit so the doctors fixed my neck up in bandages and a little bit of glue since it was a bad open wound. It was just slightly cut open. It was open enough for doctors and nurses to hold it shut with the glue. I never could remember how or why I crashed. All I could remember was driving around in big parking lot of a convenience store with my friends from school smoking cigerettes and acting like fools before school started .

(Proverbs 18:2) "A fool takes no pleasure in understanding, but only in expressing his opinion."

(Proverbs 14:15) "The simple believes everything, but the prudent gives thought to his steps."

These verses explain that a wise person will examine things carefully, before that person makes a decision. A person needs to understand the risks and rewards before that person choses a course of action. A person who acts like a fool does not rely on hope or anything God has to offer. By acting like a fool a person continues to take action towards their understanding rather than God's. The next thing I realize is that I'm smacked right into a pole and then sent to the hospital for treatment.   The doctors said I must have blacked out somehow during the impact. They found no trace of alcohol in my system. I was just indeed acting foolish sobor. With the medical condition I was born with, a lot of this could have caused me to black out like panic attacks, high levels of anxiety, seizures, high phenylalanine levels. In biblical terms a controlling spirit that is attached to someone, is now controlled through manipulation and deceit. Behind every person that operates in manipulation is a spirit of control. All because I had allowed the manipulation of that controlling spirit into my life through Trinity. Evil spirits can be transfered from person to person through the sin of others and those who accept that persons sin by the mirror image of doing that sinful act yourself. When we allow that controlling spirit to operate in our lives we will always seek preeminence. This means to surpass all others by always having to be first or being superior above all others. In the bible Paul says:

(Romans 8:5-10) "For those who live according to the flesh set their minds on the things of the flesh, but those who live according to the Spirit set their minds on the things of the Spirit. For to set the mind on the flesh is death, but to set the mind on th into bare Spirit is life and peace. For the mind that is set on the flesh is hostile to God, for it does not submit to God's law; indeed, it cannot. Those who are in the flesh cannot please God. You, however, are not in the flesh but in the Spirit, if in fact the Spirit of God dwells in you. Anyone who does not have the Spirit of Christ does not belong to him, But if Christ is in you, although the body is dead because of sin, the Spirit is life because of righteousness."

I picked up so many bad habits from Trinity.   One of the many bad habits was using a fake ID to get me inside bars. I was 17 when I started going to the bars with Trinity, and she was 22. We went to a lot of different bars near the westside. She had got me into some clubs in downtown Cleveland near the flats. That's where the real party clubs were at. By the time Trinity was 23 she became pregnant with her first by a guy she's been dating since junior high, so I came over to her place a lot to help her cause her boyfriend Greg was never there for her. He did drugs and cheated on her a lot. Of course she claimed to be so in love with him. She had a lot of trauma inflicted on her because of him. So I was trying to be the best friend I could be to her. After her son was born I even helped out with babysitting. In 2008 I turned 18 and moved out of my mom's house. I moved in at first with my brother Adam. He lived off of Madison Ave with his girlfriend Lisa. Lisa and I got along for a while. She even hooked me up with her cousin Jeremiah. He liked to be called Jeri for short. So Jeri and I dated for 6 months. Then after 6 months we broke up because he cheated on me. He cheated on me with Trinity's step sister. I was so mad at her. I said to myself if Trinity was a good friend how could she allow this to happen with my boyfriend and her step sister. Right after Jeri and I ended our relationship, I stopped talking to Trinity for a few weeks. I even stopped answering her phone calls for a little while.

Then one day she drove over to my place to show me a video that was taken the night Jeri cheated on me. The video took place at her house with everyone drunk and her step sister and Jeri together in the back room making out. More things had continued in that moment on camera. She swore she didn't know anything about the incident. Of course I felt for that one. She was such a liar! I was very naive at the time and felt for every lie she ever told me. According to the bible:

(Proverbs 17:17) "A friend loves at all times, and a brother is born for adversity."

Friends are supposed to be loving, caring, supporting one another in love. Of course Trinity was not a good loving friend. I wasn't the only one having relationship issues. Adam was having problems with Lisa. He found out she was secretly talking to another guy behind his back. So he kicked her out of the apartment. Lisa was trying to put up a fight since she didn't want to leave willingly. Adam had kindly asked her to give back the apartment keys that Adam had made for her while they were living together. When she threw the keys at Adam out of anger, I then charged after her in rage and grabbed her by the arm then smacked her and said some swear words at her while raising my voice in the process. I got so angry at her because of the way she treated my brother. She turned around and grabbed her stuff and left while slamming the door on the way out with some swear words aiming toward me. Adam grabbed me as I started walking toward the door towards Lisa with anger. She was walking out when Adam told me to just let it go. I was ready to really throw some punches out there. I wasn't ready to give up on a fight. Adam had convinced me that she wasn't worth the stress. After a while Adam had a new girlfriend named Becka. I was very depressed and crying over Jeri. Yes I was young and naive not knowing what true love really was. The bible teaches us:

(1 Corinthians 13:4-8) "Love is patient and Love is kind; love does not envy or boast, it is not arrogant or rude. It

*does not insist on its own way; it is not irritable or resentful;
it does not rejoice at wrongdoing, but rejoices with the truth."*
There are 4 types of love: romantic love, family
love, brotherly love, and God's divine love.   In the
bible Jesus says:

*(John 13:34-35) "I give you a new commandment: Love
each other, Just as I have loved you, so you also must love
each other, This is how everyone will know that you are my
disciples, when you love each other."*

So what Jesus is saying to you is that if you
welcome God's love into your heart, then you will
be able to love like God. I had problems with love
not just with men but with friends, family and people
in general because my heart was filled with anger,
disappointment, hatred, envy and Jealousy. I
thought I knew what love was but I didn't. In the
beginning of summer 2008 I graduated high school.
I moved out of my brother's apartment. I stayed
with Trinity.   My mom was mad at me for moving
out. She decided not to come to my graduation
ceremony. My mom and I stopped talking for a

while. Grandpa Clay came to my graduation ceremony with my aunt Donna and my brother Adam. After the graduation ceremony had ended we went and had dinner at grandpa Clay's house. Grandma Asa was cooking a tasty spaghetti dinner in celebration of my graduation. That was my favorite dish. Later that evening grandpa Clay took me back to Trinity's house where I was now living. Trinity had also thrown me a graduation party that night. She invited a lot of her friends and I had a few of mine too. We got drunk that late evening. I even hooked up with this boy Chris. He also wanted Trinity too. That made me mad and jealous.

(Mark 7:21-22) "For from within, out of the heart of men, proceed evil thoughts, adulteries, fornications, murders, thefts, covetousness, wickedness, deceit, lasciviousness, an evil eye, blasphemy, pride, foolishness."

Most of that was going on at this party. I seemed to be having fun at first but then I saw my ex Jeri. I asked Trinity why he was at the party and she told me she invited him. She also pulled me aside and said "we been seeing each other as friends but he likes me and I like him but I told him I didn't want anything more until I got permission from you Grace." I felt so mad and betrayed. As naive as I was I gave in and said "you can have him it's cool I'm over him any way." Even though deep down I was not ok with it nor was I really over him. I was trying to keep my popularity with Trinity. So her and Jeri ended up sleeping together that night and I had to listen to it. How it killed me inside and the more I seen them together the more upset I felt.

(Isaiah 43:18) "Forget the former things; do not dwell on the past."

I felt in my heart so much jealousy and rage that I couldn't let this go. I wanted revenge on Jeri for what he did to me. According to the bible:

(Romans 12:19) "Beloved, never avenge yourselves, but leave it to the wrath of God, for it is written, Vengeance is mine, I will repay, says the Lord."

God tells us to never take revenge and to leave it to the Lord. God is in fact the ultimate judge and when we seek revenge, we are stepping in His place.

When we become overwhelmed with what others have done wrong to us, we become filled with anger and find ourselves focused on hatred. God's love and forgiveness is seen in our ability to love and forgive.

(1 Peter 3:9) "Do not repay evil with evil or insult with insult, on the contrary, repay evil with blessings, because to this you were called so that you may inherit a blessing."

We have to act on love otherwise hatred will consume us. I held on to a lot of hatred in my past. I tried to convince Trinity into getting back together with her ex who was her son's father because she's always been in love with him even though he treated her like dirt. I didn't care, I just wanted Jeri. One night Jeri got mad at me. We started to argue. Then he almost pushed me down the stairs. That scared the living crap out of me. I had already had bad experiences with boys putting their hands on me. Then another night something happened, which really put the fear in me. Jeri had his friend Josh over and Josh had a 9mm handgun on him that night. It was like 2 or 3 in the middle of the night and I was

past out sleeping. I slept on Trinity's couch. Josh
had approached me beside the couch where I was
sleeping with his 9mm handgun. He then put the
gun behind my head. My head was turned to the
side facing the wall that the couch was up against. I
was then startled when he covered my mouth with
his hand saying in my ear while whispering to me
and his finger on the trigger "If you mess with
Trinity and Jeri's relationship again I will pull this
trigger." He told me he would have pulled that
trigger right then and there. He claimed he had
respect for Trinity and her baby. If that were true he
would have never come into the house with the gun
on him in the first place. I was so scared that night.
Fear was just taking over my spirit.

(Deuteronomy 3:22) "You shall not fear them, for it is
the Lord your God who fights for you."

Jesus teaches us:

(Matthew 10:28) "Do not fear those who kill the body but
cannot kill the soul but rather to fear Him who can destroy
both soul and body in hell."

There are three types of fear: Rational fear, primal fear, and irrational fear. Rational fears occur when there is a real, imminent threat like when Josh pulled out his gun on me. Primal fear is defined as an innate fear that is programmed into our brains such as fear in our ways of thinking or hallucinations that the mind makes up. Irrational fears are the ones that don't make logical sense and can vary greatly from person to person.

(2 Timothy 1:7) "God has not given us the spirit of fear, but of power, and of love, and of a sound mind."

This scripture explains to us that it is a sin to walk in fear. When we invite Jesus in our lives we can overcome any spirit of fear. In time these were things I had to overcome because fear had gotten the best of me. After a while since this incident had happened I finally moved on. I then started dating Jeri's other friend Chuck. Chuck seemed nice for a little while till one night Trinity's attractive friend Tara came over and Chuck started getting the hots for her. They were talking and went outside for a cigarette. They were gone for over an hour and I began to be worried. I went outside walking toward Trinity's backyard and before my eyes I saw chuck with Tara on the back porch getting intimate with each other. I ran back in the house with tears of anger falling down my face. I grabbed my pack of cigarettes and smoked a few on the front porch. Trinity came out behind me to see what was going on pretending to be a caring friend that she wasn't. So I told her what had happened. She told me when they come back inside the house that I should fight Tara. Trinity and Tara were so two faced they both pretend to be each other's friends. Then they talk behind each others back. Someone who seems to be two faced according to the bible is known as being double minded.

(James 1:8) "He is a double minded man, unstable in all his ways."

Someone who is double minded and or two faced means that they are not sincere, saying unpleasant things about you to other people while seeming to be pleasant when that same someone is around you. When they came back in the house words started flying out of my mouth at her. She then pushed and shoved me. I grabbed her and dragged her down to the floor with full rage of anger. We both began pushing each other. We found ourselves wrestling each other on the floor. Trinity was enjoying the show for a while as she was amused by our fighting and arguing. She then eventually broke up the fight to have us make up. She got tired of watching us fight after a while. After that night I did not trust Tara again. Somehow we did become friends again. Although she wasn't really a friend nor did she act like one. One minute were both nice to each others faces. As soon as our backs were turned she ran her mouth about me. I ran my mouth about her even though back then I didn't realize two wrongs don't make a right. I had a lot of hatred toward her. I felt that I had to put up with her, for the popularity. She got mad at me one night when I took revenge by sleeping with her friend Aj. I just wanted to get back at someone whether it was Trinity or Tara I didn't care. There was so much anger and hate stirring up inside me.

(Matthew 18:15) "If your brother sins against you, go and tell him his fault, between you and him alone, if he listens to you, you have gained your brother."

This verse states if someone sins against you, you need to address them first not another person. Getting even is not the right way to go about the problem. God teaches us to forgive, and let go. I didn't know how to do that at the time. I fell into a deeper, and dark place from everything that was going on with me. I had troubles with friends who I thought cared about me. I was so wrong. I had mistakes with boys, I thought I was so in love with. I felt so self conscious, and had a lot of hatred toward myself and others. In my heart I felt torn, used and abused. I thought to myself while sitting on the porch with a cigarette in my mouth. In my mind I felt that Brandon was the only one that stuck around so long I should go back to try to make it work with him. That night I called Brandon because I seemed desperate in finding love in all the wrong places. It seems like when we hate ourselves we struggle with hatred towards how we look, how we feel, what we've done, what's been done to us, or what we keep failing to accomplish in our lives.

(Ephesians 1:4) "Even before he made the world, God loved us and chose us in Christ to be holy and without fault in his eye."

People may hate themselves because of the things they,ve done in their past or they might hate themselves due to something they may be currently struggling with such as an addiction or an unhealthy relationship. When our minds and lives are steeped, in truth, there is no room for self-hatred. God's word teaches us:

(Genesis 1:27) "So God created man in his own image, in the image of God created him; male and female he created them."

We are all beautifully made perfect in God's own image. That is why there is no room for self hatred because God sees the beauty in all his creation. I wasn't thinking like that yet the darkness kept building up inside my spirit causing my soul to have an unclean spirit.

(Mark 1:23) "And there was in their synagogue a man with an unclean spirit; and he cried out."

An unclean spirit also known as a demonic spirit is caused by multiple traumatic events that may have occurred in a persons life causing an invisible door to be open for demonic spirits. Once that door is opened, then it allows that spirit to try and take full control over any situation. I had enough of Trinity with her lies with her controlling spirit. I got back with Brandon then moved out of Trinity's place once and for all. I just couldn't take it anymore.

Chapter 8
The Road to An unclean Spirit
Part One:

It was the middle of summer in 2008. Brandon and I got back together. I lived on the westside in an apartment with him and his mom. I moved out of Trinity's place. I just could not take the torment of her actions toward me any more. A month later I rode with Brandon down to Orlando Florida to stay with his Aunt and Uncle. We stayed down there for 2 months to help his family move back to Buffalo New York where Brandon and his family were from. While in Florida my mom called me up one day saying my biological father was living in Miami Florida. I then took an interest in searching for my dad. I was very anxious to meet him. I went through the phonebook to look up the number of were he was still working after 30 years. To my surprise he picked up the phone. We briefly spoke since I was too nervously afraid in what to say to him after all these years I didn't know him. At that moment we were both eager to meet each other. Brandon and I took a trip to Miami to meet him. We pulled up to a corner bar near the beach where he was working. I was so nervous and asked myself will he accept me or deny me? Does he even want anything to do with me? I sat in the car for a few minutes asking myself these questions. I didn't feel like getting out of the car at that moment. I felt too nervous and worried. Nervousness can be hard to deal with. According to the bible in every situation we are to ask God for his strength and encouragement. He will give us comfort by relying on the power of the Holy spirit.

(Philippians 4:6-7) "Be anxious for nothing, but in everything by prayer and supplication, with thanksgiving, let your requests be made known to God; and the peace of God, which surpasses all understanding, will guard your hearts and minds through Christ Jesus."

Nervousness can be overcomed by believing in the blood of Jesus. At this time my belief had fallen away from me. I was a nervous wreck at this time not knowing in my mind of how to handle this situation. I soon came to my senses and finally stepped out the car. In my heart I knew I just had to meet him. I was at the age of 18 years old when I finally met my dad for the first time. He was hispanic from South America. He lived in Miami Florida for 20 years. His name was Louie Gomez. At this time he was very fluent in his English with hardly any spanish accent left. I briefly spoke with him on the phone. Seeing him for the first time I finally put a face to his voice from the phone. He was actually very excited to meet me. We ended up talking in person for a few hours and had dinner together. It was such a blessing for both of us to finally meet each other. I was so happy to have met my dad. Over time we built a great relationship. I believe God had brought us both together to come to know each other in restoration. Restoration is the renewing of our hearts, wounds, broken families, and our returning from sin, and returning to God.

(1 Peter 5:10) "And after you have suffered a little while, the God of all grace, who has called you to his eternal glory in Christ, will himself restore, confirm, strengthen, and establish you."

As believers in Christ Jesus he calls us out from our sufferings into his glorious kingdom. There were more things about to take place along the road. It felt great to meet my dad for the first time. When the day ended Brandon and I then traveled with his Uncle. We met up with a friend of his in Tampa Florida. Brandon's uncle's friend was a big drug dealer in the Tampa area. We bought some drugs off of him. One night we all were taking some heavy drugs.   I was up all night. I slept the whole day away soon after that. I smoked a lot back then while using hard core drugs. Eventually I did become addicted to those drugs. Addictions can take over the spirit because it affects the body, mind and soul.

(1 John 2:16) "For everything in the world, the lust of the flesh, the lust of the eyes, and the pride of life, comes not from the father but from the world."

An addiction is the fact or condition of being addicted to a particular substance, thing, or activity. Addictions can cause chronic stress and or mental illness. People may feel like taking drugs help there problems, but in reality it actually causes more problems. In my mind, it was a method of coping with everything I've been through. Little did I know, it was only making things worse for me. As the two months went by it was time to leave Orlando and head up to Buffalo New York. Before leaving with Brandon and his family, I said goodbye to my dad as we hugged. We both shed some heart-felt tears from meeting each other for the first time. He didn't want me to leave. He knew I had a life back in Cleveland Ohio that I had to soon get back to. Eventually we ended up making it to Buffalo, New York. Brandon and I went to a friends house in Queens to play poker and drink. We were taking drugs that same night also. Brandon and I were hanging out with our friends in Queens, New York. I was living in Buffalo at this time for a few months until I got a phone call from my mom saying that my aunt had passed away. That's when I made my way back to Cleveland with Brandon for my aunt's

funeral.

Chapter 9
The Road to An Unclean Spirit
Part Two:

It was still the year of 2008 and summer had not quite ended yet when I got the news that my aunt passed away. Brandon and I packed up our stuff and headed back up to Ohio. Unfortunately, Brandon and I realized we had nowhere to go when we came back to Ohio. We couldn't stay with his mom cause she got remarried and only shared a small one bedroom apartment. My mom and I were still not on speaking terms, ever since I moved out. My mother and I were both angry. We both were filled with hatred toward one another. According to the bible:

(Exodus 20:12) "Honor your father and mother, that your days may be long in the land that the Lord your God is giving you."

We're supposed to love, honor and obey our parents. By honoring your parents its a blessing from God that you may live a long and happy life. I was breaking that commandment by dispising my mom. I was bitter towards her. When we went to my aunt's funeral my mother and I didn't speak at all. I was happy to see my grandparents. I introduced Brandon to them at my aunts funeral. My mom and grandpa Clay got into an argument because of her attitude towards me. She made it clear to me that she wanted nothing to do with me. I didn't want anything to do with her either.

(Deuteronomy 27:16) "Cursed be anyone who dishonors his father or his mother. And all the people shall say, Amen!"

What does it mean to dishonor your parents? It simply means to despise them in your heart. In my heart I did despise my mother. We didn't make any contact with each other at the funeral. We only made negative facial expressions to one another.

(Proverbs 30:17) "The eye that mocks a father and despises a mother's instructions will be plucked out by ravens of the valley and eaten by vultures."

If someone does not learn to obey and honor their parents it shows dishonorment to them and to the Lord our God. God hates irreverent looks, gestures, and attitudes towards parents. God loves us enough to forgive. At this time I didn't have it in me to honor my mother or show her any love. After the funeral ended we departed and all went our separate ways. Brandon talked to an old high school friend of his, Kevin. He talked about staying at his place since we had nowhere else to go. He said it'll take him some time to get a spot opened in his house for us. Then for a few weeks after my aunt's funeral we slept in Brandon's car homeless for a little bit. Then as weeks passed his friend Kevin called him back and said we can move in a spot he had opened up to us in his basement on Broadway Avenue East side of Cleveland. I got a part time job working at Burger King down the street so I walked to and from work. Days I had off, we all hung out to drink and smoke

and watch football and basketball games. Brandon
and I stayed at his friend's house for the next 3
months till I had saved up for Brandon and I to get
our own place together. We moved out of his
friend's house and moved into a place back over on
the west part of Cleveland. It was on W 85th on the
corner of Trisket. A few friends of ours moved in
too. Brandon's friend Tj, and my friend Elena had
started living with us for a short time. Tj was a drug
dealer and eventually we became part of that by
selling drugs to people we knew off the streets. We
made money fast with Tj as our supplier. We were
always inviting people over to our place to hang
with us and drink. We smoked in the attic a lot when
we had a house full of our friends over. Trinity
came over one night. I still hung out with Trinity
occasionally. I don't know why but I still remained
friends with Trinity. I babysat a lot for her and her
sister Danisha. One night I went to Danisha's house
to babysit while Brandon stayed home to hangout
with his friends. Danisha and her husband along
with Trinity and her boyfriend went out to the club

as I stayed behind to watch their kids one night. I watched movies and played games with the kids then sat down to have dinner with them. After that I tucked them into bed after reading a story to them. I then began yawning and getting sleepy after the long evening with the kids. I cracked open a couple wine coolers after the kids were passed out. I soon passed out on Danisha's couch while watching a movie. It was about 3am in the morning when by surprise I was awoken out of a deep sleep to who I thought was Brandon on top of me. Then after my eyes being adjusted after a deep sleep I then realized it was not Brandon at all. It was Danisha's husband. I then snapped out of it being awoken in immediate fear. I then realized he had no clothes on. He covered my mouth for a brief moment. Then put his finger against his lips assuring me to stay quiet. He then started to place his hands up under my shirt. With a panic of fear inside me I pushed him and as drunk as he was, he fell right off the couch and passed out. I leaped right off the couch then ran outside. I quickly grabbed my cell phone to start

calling Brandon to come pick me up from Danisha's
house. He answered right away and could hear the
fear in my voice. I explained to him what had
happened. He told me to call Danisha and wait for
him outside. I didn't dare go back in the house. I
remained outside to wait for Brandon to come get
me. Meanwhile, I called Danisha and told her and
Trinity what had happened. Danisha started crying
over the phone after hearing what her husband had
tried to do to me. Danisha and Trinity arrive back
after Brandon pulls into the driveway. We talked
about the incident for an hour outside while smoking
a cigarette. I felt bad for Danisha and the things she
was going though with her and her husband. She
had told me that this wasn't the first time he's tried
cheating on her. According to Danisha, she's not
surprised. He's tried many times to cheat on her.
This is the first time he was caught in action.
Danisha's other friends have tried telling her about
her husband's actions. She refused to believe them,
until now. Soon after we talked I got into the car
with Brandon and we began to drive back to our

place. After our long conversation about what had happened, I felt as if they had thought I had done something wrong, even though I came forward about what happened. I just cried and cried all the way back home. Trinity was acting like a police officer and started to interrogate me with her questions. Somehow I felt she did not believe me. I felt betrayed and all alone.

(Proverbs 11:9) "With his mouth the godless man would destroy his neighbor, but by knowledge the righteous are delivered."

What this means is that when a person gives false statements and accusations, even when a person doesn't believe the truth about the situation and questions that person out of disbelief, this can cause the person who is being falsely accused to become angry and inscure being doubtful of oneself. More importantly, being falsely accused of wrongdoing of any kind may lead you to experience intense high levels of emotional trauma that may impact your life in different aspects. When your wrongly accused or being questioned constantly about your actions and motives, it can lead to emotional abuse. One of the ten commandments in the bible says:

(Exodus 20:16) "You shall not bear false witness to your neighbor."

The nineth commandment out of the ten commandments of God specifies that a person can't present false statements against another person otherwise punishment with judgement shall be upon them. This verse is a perfect example of false witnessing:

(Matthew 26:59) "Now the chief priests and the whole council were seeking false testimony against Jesus that they might try to put him to death."

I couldn't sleep that night so I stayed up. I smoked since that was my only way of coping with problems at the time. Soon after that Trinity and I fell away from each other for a little while. Brandon and I continued hanging out with our other friends and doing drugs. I tried not to think about what had happened at Danisha's house but it was hard when Trinity made me feel like the bad guy even though I felt like I didn't do anything wrong. I told her the truth about the incident and I still felt like I was being accused of doing something wrong. In my mind getting high or drunk was the only way I delt with pain at this time. This is how I would put my mind at ease of my many traumas of my past. I still struggled with my faith. I would still cry myself to sleep sometimes. My mind at this point was only getting darker. I was even further away from God's love.

Chapter 10
The Darkening of The Mind

    It was now the end of summer and fall was just beginning. I ran into an old friend of mine his name was Thomas. Thomas was a good friend of mine at the time. We smoked and drank a lot together at our house parties that Brandon and I had. One night Thomas came by the house to pick up an order he had placed over the phone with TJ. Brandon and I gave him the hook up. We went out on the porch to smoke a cigarette. Thomas then suggested to me that I should work at a gentlemen's night club. I laughed, feeling very insecure of myself. He assured me that I could make a lot of money working in that type of work. Thomas had explained to me the beautiful young woman that I was even though I felt insecure of myself. I just continued to laugh filled with doubt and shame in myself. I then agreed to try out this new experience that Thomas explained to me was a good idea. He then drove me to the nightclub later that night, a place called Kristy's Cabaret. The owner asked me if I would like to audition on stage that night. He said they needed more girls in the nightclub. I was shy, and so very insecure of my body. I did it anyway with Thomas assuring me that everything was going to be fine and instead of following God's plan for me I decided to follow my own path which eventually led me down a dark road. Little did I know that this was my fall away from what I believed in as a christian. Things would soon get worse for me down the road.

(1 Corinthians 10:13) "No temptation has overtaken you except such as is common to man; but God is faithful, who will not allow you to be tempted beyond what you are able, but with the temptation will also make the way of escape, that you may be able to bear it."

We as humans wrestle against the dark spirits of this world driving us to fall into temptation and lies coming from the evil one. At this time my faith was very weak. Instead of walking in the spirit I was indeed walking in the flesh. Then the owner watched me audition and soon after he asked me if I could start the next day. I got all excited as I said yes. I was so desperate to make money that I didn't care how I would make the money. I worked six days a week. The night club soon became my new life. Brandon liked the idea of me working at the nightclub. Thomas told him about how I could make a lot of money and get handed a more supply of drugs. My first night at the club, the bartender had explained to me that the more drinks the guys buy me the more money I can make. By the end of the night, I had many guys buying me shots that night. I came home every night being intoxicated or high from drugs.

(1 Timothy 6:10) "The love of money is the root of all evil."

It is through this craving that some have wandered away from the faith and pierced themselves with many sorrows. Money can be used for good. In this specific verse it explains that lusting after money, and the increasing desire to gain more money to increase worldly wealth, draws people farther away from God's love. This takes a person deeper into temptation through the hardships of this world. I didn't realize I was falling into the devil's trap. This is his way of holding me down and getting inside my mind. Of course I being weak in my faith allowed him to do so. I then proceeded to do things through the lust of my flesh. I was walking to work one night with my high heels on, wearing a long jacket over my work outfit. A black cadillac soon pulled up beside me. As I was walking, an older man yelled out to me to get in the car, assuring me that it was safe to proceed. I didn't know what to expect at that moment when I proceeded to get into the vehicle. In my mind I just needed to get to work someway, somehow. As he was driving, he soon began touching my leg moving up to my inner thigh. At that moment I felt very nervous and worried because of the attacks that happened to me when I was younger in the past. I was so afraid to speak up for myself. The man pulled up in the back parking lot of the night club, where we were out of sight. He soon began to touch himself in an inappropriate way. He locked the door and told me I wasn't aloud to leave until I had finished my job. I was very confused and scared. I knew I wasn't going any where until I did what he told me to do. Then after the evil deed was done he threw cash at me then sent me on my way. At that moment I felt ashamed of myself. In my mind I did what I had to do to survive as scared as I was. I had no idea what that man could've been capable of. I'm glad God was able to get me out of that situation. That night I was talking to one of the girls that I work with, about what happened. The girl took me to the bathroom to do a few lines of illegal drugs with her. I felt in my mind that doing the drugs would help numb the pain that I was feeling inside. Jesus said:

(John 14:27) "I do not give to you as the world gives, Do not let your hearts be troubled and do not be afraid."

Sometimes an unexpected pain or illness may frighten you. Accept God's gift of peace, and let it create a calm spirit within you. God provides peace when you ask for it. If you ever had a mind like mine that was dark and cloudy, it's kind of hard to think about God's peace. I let my lusts and temptations of this world take control over my life instead of allowing God to take control of it. One night I was talking to a customer and he wanted me to go with him back to this motel. He grabbed me by the hand and assured me that everything would be alright. At this time nothing I was doing was alright. I went with the man back to his motel room. He insisted on me pleasuring him with his lustful desires. When the evil deed was completed he gave me a lump of cash. Then he took me and dropped me off by the corner of where I stayed. When I got home, I then went to the attic to smoke some herbs with Brandon and his friends. Once again I wanted to numb the pain that I was feeling inside.

(Ephesians 2:3) "Among them we too all formerly lived in the lusts of our flesh, indulging the desires of the flesh and of the mind, and were by nature children of wrath, even as the rest."

Every person is marked with sin, both deliberate and accidental, and for this reason we deserve to be separated from God. We are all born sinners. The default position of every human life is that we are under the wrath of God. The impulse to sin runs in the bloodlines of people of every race. We live in sin, in our actions and our thoughts. When it means to be children of wrath it simply means we're under God's judgment. We are subject to His judgments. There is a judgment that exists upon all who truly do not know Christ. This is why we are called to believe in Jesus by the grace of God through faith.

(Ephesians 2:8-9) "For by grace you have been saved through faith, and this is not your own doing; it is the gift of God, not a result of works, so that no one may boast." Seek to share him with others worldwide. God's gift is given to all mankind. I still srtuggled with my faith. My mind was still clouded with much darkness. Some nights when I worked, I decided to give free private dances in exchange for drugs. One night after giving some guy a private dance, I went into the girls bathroom and noticed a white, sticky substance on my back. The guy I was giving a private dance to had ejaculated on me without me

even knowing. I was so upset I went to the girls bathroom feeling utterly disgusted with myself. I was so ashamed I couldn't even wrap my head around it. I was angry at this man for what he had done. I was mostly angry with myself. One night I left the club with a friend of mine from work. We drove out to the eastside where she stayed to pick up more drugs. Her and I were up all night driving around town to hustle up some more money to purchase more drugs from some old friends of hers. We stopped at a few corners. She jumped in a few other vehicles at each stop to make some quick cash. I had no idea what we were getting ourselves into at this point in time. I did anything to get drugs because in my mind it helped numb the pain that I was feeling. It didnt really take away all the pain because the pain I had deep inside of me was still there. Other nights in the club I would get taken advantage of and not even realize it. I left one night with two guys. I didn't know them very well. I went with them anyway. They took me back to their place. One threw me on the bed with force then

began to have his way with me. Then the other
pushed him aside to proceed to do the same thing. I
layed there on the bed lifeless not knowing why I
was doing what I was doing. At this time I gave up
on fighting and allowed them to pursue their dirty
actions on me. My mind was in a dark place at this
time. I felt so lost and distant from the love of God.
I was ashamed of myself with disappointment. I
felt that drugs were the only way of dealing with
pain at this time. I left as they handed me cash while
walking out the door. I cried on my way home that
night. I was walking home smoking a cigerette. I
felt very lost in this corrupted world not really
understanding that I could be yet found again
through Christ. When I gave my life to christ a fews
years back, I didn't realize that I needed to give him
my whole heart and mind. I was still living with all
the trauma of my past.

(Matthew 11:28-29) "Come to me, all you who are weary
and burdened, and I will give you rest, for I am gentle and
humble in heart, and you will find rest for your souls. For my
yoke is easy and my burden is light."

Many times we feel overwhelmed with the burdens we carry in this life. God has promised us that we can find strength in him, and he will provide rest for us.

(Philippians 4:13) "I can do all things through Christ Jesus who gives me strength."

Unfortunately at this point in time, I had no strength. There were many more problems that were still yet to come my way. It was a cold winter in December of 2008. I was on my way to work the next day when I arrived. I seen this new girl I had barely known. I remember seeing her around in school. She just got hired as a new dancer. She was already starting drama with some of the other girls. I tried minding my own business at first. Then I went straight up to the dressing room to get ready for the night. As I came down from the dressing room she walked up to me and got in my face saying I stole her wallet. I thought to myself "why is she accusing me of doing something like that? I barely knew the girl." I was starting to fill up with rage and hatred toward this girl. I took her up to the girls dressing room just to strip myself of all my clothing to prove to her that I did not take her wallet. I even emptied out my purse of everything I had in there to show her I didn't have her wallet. She still accused me of stealing after everything I did to prove her wrong. Then the night started and customers were coming in as she was still starting her drama with me. The rage was really building up inside of me. I had already had a few drinks that night. I smoked in the girls dressing room while I was getting ready for the night. I then saw her with a customer as I heard her begin to gossip about me stealing her wallet.

(Proverbs 6:16-19) "There are six things the Lord hates, seven that are an abomination to him: haughty eyes, a lying tongue, and hands that shed innocent blood, a heart that devises wicked plans, feet that make haste to run to evil, a false witness who breathes out lies, and one who sows discord among brothers."

An abomination is something that causes extreme disgust and intense loathing. A person who allows his or her heart to remain sinful and to devise wicked schemes will ultimately run into sinful acts if given the opportunity. Our actions will be accountable in the days of judgment. If we learn to repent, and turn back to God, we will then see brighter days during judgment. All these negative conflicts will lead to a broken spirit, which has a great impact on our hearts, thoughts and feelings. To be crushed in the spirit simply means to have a tendency to harm yourself or others around you because of the traumatic incidents of ones past.

(Isaiah 43:18) "Forget the former things; do not dwell on the past."

God doesn't want us to dwell on the past. In this time of my story, I held on to a lot of things from my past that I just didn't understand how to let go. Learning to let go was difficult for me. I then walked up to her, with a force of rage I pushed her with a shove and began to yell out curse words at her. A customer graded me to hold me back because I was ready to take her down with full rage. Two men were in between us to keep us from fighting. In my mind I was ready for a fight to the finish. I wasn't ready to give up on this fight. I felt the rage inside me about to be unleashed. As she started to walk away the two men that were keeping us from fighting slowly started to walk away. I saw my opportunity to make my move on her. With full rage I grabbed the first thing I saw which was a steel chair. I picked it up over my head, then threw it toward her with full force. The bouncer jumped in front of her to keep the chair from hurting her. Instead the chair ended up hitting him. As he was in critical condition security had asked me to leave or they were going to call the police on me for assault charges. I agreed to leave. I then left the club that night full of anger. I felt bad for what I did to the bouncer. Still filled with rage and torment inside, I was still seeking my revenge on her. I got her number from a friend at work. I was calling and texting her. I was determined to get even with her.

(Leviticus 19:18) "Do not seek revenge or bear a grudge against anyone among your people, but love your neighbor as yourself, I am the Lord."

According to this scripture we are not to bear grudges against one another but simply repay evil with good. God tells us to never take revenge and to leave it to the Lord. God is the ultimate judge. When we seek revenge, we act on taking his place. When we become overwhelmed with what others have done wrong, we become more focused on hate. God's love and forgiveness is seen in our ability to love and forgive. At this point on my journey I still had a lot to learn from all these events that had occurred throughout my past. The first step was learning to forgive and let go of the nightmares from my past.

Chapter 11
The Girl With The Scarlet letter

As the months went by after being escorted by security out of the club, I spent more time with Brandon at our place. Elena moved out into her new boyfriend's apartment. TJ decided to go stay with one of his friends for a while. That left Brandon and I the place all to ourselves. During a doctor's appointment it was revealed to me that my blood work had indicated that I was pregnant. I told my mom about the news. She was shocked at first, then she accepted the fact that she was going to be a grandma for the first time. I told Adam and he was happy he was going to be an uncle. I had just turned 19 years old. I was so excited to hear I was going to be a mom. I explained to my grandparents the exciting news. The doctor had determined that I was only 2 weeks into the pregnancy. With my medical condition Dr. Sue Jackson had explained to me the complications that could happen to me and the baby during the pregnancy. She explained that I was a high risk pregnancy. A high risk pregnancy is when a woman and her unborn child face a higher than normal chance of experiencing complications during, or after pregnancy. Complications also could occur during delivery. I was very scared and nervous with everything that she said could happen to me or the baby. These were all possibilities that can be prevented. She then explained to me what possible things I could do in order to prevent the possibility of complacations with me or the baby. My first instinct was to get on my knees to pray to God, that me and my baby would be fine and healthy.

(Matthew 19:26) "With man it is impossible, but with God all things are possible."

I had to learn how to trust that God was going to work out everything for my good. My faith soon began small like a mustard seed.

(Matthew 17:20) He said to them, "Because of your little faith, for truly, I say to you, if you have faith like a grain of

mustard seed, you will say to that mountain, move from here to there, and it will move, and nothing will be impossible for you."

With faith like a mustard seed, I began to get myself together by quitting smoking, not doing anymore drugs, or drinking. I was determined to be completely sober throughout my pregnancy. I heard from one of my friends that Trinity was also pregnant again with her second baby. We began to see each other again, despite everything she put me through. I was so focused on preparing for my baby to arrive. I started going back to church. Brandon had come along with me a few times. I was too afraid to tell anyone at church about the pregnancy. My church believed in marriage before baby making. I felt deeply ashamed, yet very excited to meet my new baby. I couldn't wait to become a mother. I started going to teen pregnancy classes that my doctor had suggested to me in downtown Cleveland. I got sick the first two months of my pregnancy. I went through some bad withdrawals too. I managed to get through the withdrawals after a few months. It took a lot of strength for me to get through the first few months of my pregnancy.

(Isaiah 40:29) "He gives strength to the weary and increases the power of the weak."

We grow tired and weary in our faith sometimes. The Lord promises to provide strength for us in our time of need. I believe he was there for me when I needed him but didn't quite know it yet. My faith was still weak. I was still a new babe in the spirit. I still didn't understand God's plan for me yet. I was soon 5 months pregnant and had a small baby bump. I then found out the gender of my baby. It was a boy! I was amazed seeing the ultrasound pictures. I felt so blessed to be a mother of a soon to be baby boy. I felt little kicks from time to time which was a true blessing from God. For the first time in my traumatic life, I've felt joy I've never felt before thanks be to God. I even had a cat that was overprotective of me during my pregnancy. I didn't realize at the time that God was really looking out for me, and my baby in ways I didn't understand.

(Matthew 19:13-15) Then little children were brought to Jesus for him to place his hands on them and pray for them. Jesus said "Let the little children come to me, and do not hinder them, for the kingdom of Heaven belongs to such as these."

Every child is a blessing from the Lord. It is up to us as parents to love, cherish and provide nourishment for that child. I was determined to give my child a better life than I was living. I knew in that moment when I felt butterfly kicks from him that I had a deep love for my child. It was so precious only a mother could understand as Mary did with Jesus.

(Psalm 139:13-14) "For you formed my inward parts; you knitted me together in my mother's womb. I praise you, for I am fearfully and wonderfully made. Wonderful are your works; my soul knows it very well."

God creates children before they are physically born. Every single person is a masterpiece unto the Lord because we are beautifully made in his image. Jesus is that perfect example of that image because he is

God in the flesh who brings forth the word which is life and truth that is why Jesus says:

> *(John 14:6) "I am the way the truth and the life no one gets to the father except through me."*

This was a wonderful feeling I had and loved thanking God, cherishing every moment of it. At 6 months of my pregnancy things started going downhill. I found out I had gestational diabetes and I really needed to watch what I was eating. Doctor Sue gave me a very specific diet to stick too. I also had to check my blood sugar 3 times a day. This was the part of my pregnancy that I really had a struggle with. I soon began to rapidly gain weight. Diabetes during pregnancy can be caused by high sugar levels in the blood during pregnancy. This is called gestational diabetes in which the mother and the baby's health could be affected at high risk during pregnancy. After delivery the blood sugar returns to is normal levels. However it is possible to develop type 2 diabetes later on in life from previously having diabetes during pregnancy. I soon did what I had to do to keep me and my baby healthy. God was by my side even when I didn't know, giving me the strength that I needed to keep believing in the safety and health of both me and my child. As a first time mother I was ready to do anything to provide a good life for my child. I was on and off going back to church. There were times even at church I felt the presence of the enemy lurking around. People at church knew I wasn't married and very young at the time. They seemed ready to point fingers to gossip about my pregnancy out of wedlock. The bible teaches us that our tongue has great power whether we use it for words of wisdom in blessing others, or words that destroy the spirit.

(James 3:6) "The tongue also is a fire, a world of evil among the parts of the body. It corrupts the whole body, sets the whole course of one's life on fire, and is itself set on fire by hell."

We should always choose our words wisely just like the saying. Words have a deep impact on people's lives. People that gossip whether its in church or outside of the church, don't seem to understand how it may bring a big impact on others. That is why we need to enable ourselves to use our tongues to encourage others. Words of encouragement is for blessing others, rather than bringing someone down with hurtful words or gossip because of the mistakes we make in life. I felt like the girl with the scarlet letter ready to be stoned for my sins I had committed.

(John 8:7) And as they continued to ask him, he stood up and said to them, "Let him who is without sin among you be the first to throw a stone at her."

We as humans are far from perfect because were sinners. Jesus was without sin and was made perfect. There was woman who was about to be stoned for her sin. Jesus had forgiven her by saying "Go and sin no more."

John 8:10-11) Jesus stood up and said to her, "Woman, where are they? Has no one, condemned you?" She said, "No one, Lord." And Jesus said, "Neither do I condemn you; go, and from now on sin no more."

Jesus is just, ready to forgive when we welcome him
into our hearts. God loves us so much he shows
love, mercy, and has compassion on us all. I believe
the Lord understood my mistakes and was always
willing to forgive, the more I opened up my heart to
Him. The further along I was, the more I was
preparing myself for my baby to arrive in this world.
Brandon and I met with the Pastor about having my
baby shower at the church. He said no because my
baby is out of wedlock. I also heard the pastor
talking to some deacons and deaconesses about my
situation.   I was so upset, I left crying thinking to
my self I know what I did was wrong. For them to
be so hateful and unkind, drove me away from my
faith once again. I thought to myself how could
these people I thought loved me, whom I trusted
betray me like this. Just as Jesus was betrayed to his
friend Judas whom he thought loved him as well.

*(Mark 14:44-46) Now the betrayer had given them a
sign, saying,"The one I will kiss is the man. Seize him and
lead him away under guard." And when he came, he went up*

up to him at once and said, "Rabbi!" And he kissed him. And they laid hands on him and seized him.

(Matthew 7:1-5) Jesus says to his disciples "Judge not, that you be not judged, For with the judgment you pronounce you will be judged, and with the measure you use it will be measured to you. Why do you see the speck that is in your brother's eye, but do not notice the log that is in your own eye? Or how can you say to your brother, Let me take the speck out of your eye, when there is a log in your own eye? You hypocrite, first take the log out of your own eye, and then you will see clearly to take the speck out of your brother's eye."

Jesus teaches us not to judge other people because they will be judged according to the same standards they use to criticize others. Jesus warns us about the significance of hypocrisy in seeing the flaw in another, or the sin while ignoring the obvious sin in our own lives. Jesus always made it clear to us that judging was to be done by the Father, and humans should concern themselves with making their own soul ready for judgement according to each individual's good works.

(Ephesians 2:10) "For we are his workmanship, created in Christ Jesus for good works, which God prepared beforehand, that we should walk in them."

I soon stopped going to church after a while. I found somewhere else to celebrate the joy of my son's arrival. We then had prepared the baby shower at a house belonging to a friend of Brandon's mom. As we were preparing for the baby shower I was on the phone talking to grandpa Clay and grandma Asa. They were getting ready to come to the baby shower along with my aunt Donna. My mom, my sisters and my brothers Cory and Adam all came too. I was happy to see my siblings. Some of my friends were able to make it to the shower. I was about 8 months pregnant when I had my baby shower. We played baby shower games and socialized with each other. The joy of my soon to be born son, was truly a blessing from the Lord. This was the start of my happiness that God has blessed me with. After the baby shower had ended Brandon and I then got back to our place. I received a disturbing phone call from Ruth's friend Juanita about how her brother Antonio had overdosed on oxycodone. They found him that night laying on the floor next to his bed. The EMT had pronounced him dead at the scene. I was so discouraged when I heard the news about his tragic death from Juanita. Sometimes we ask ourselves this big question: Why does God allow this to happen? God allows tragedy to be a warning about judgment rather than executing wrath on all sinners. Tragedies can cause a range of responses such as fear, rage, confusion, and sorrow. In our suffering, we are heartbroken and sometimes feel abandoned by God. The truth is Jesus understands suffering better than we do.

(John 3:17) "God did not send the Son into the world to condemn the world, but in order that the world might be saved through him."

Jesus sacrificed himself for us on the cross, he took the punishment for all our sins. Suffering is in our lives because we are living in a broken world. Some suffering is due to our sinful and wrong choices, but some is due to the world being fallen. Suffering happens as a warning to our poor choices we make, and as a result would be a wake up call to our spirit. In that moment, I could tell Juanita was upset and I too started shedding tears. My sister and I were very close to her and her family. A lot of mixed emotions was filling up inside of me, along with pregnancy hormones raging. I had an argument with Brandon that night cause all he could think about was getting high with his friends. So I left for a few nights to stay with my friend Kesha and her sister Alicia over on the Eastside where they now lived. I felt sick that night and Brandon was calling my cell phone all night. I choose to ignor all his phone calls. I was still 8 months into my pregnancy as I was battling with my emotions. I felt depressed and Kesha and her sister tried to be entertaining with music and dancing, I just wasn't into it. So much was running through my mind in those few days. I had lost a friend, Brandon and I were arguing all the time. While I'm trying to stay sober throughout my pregnancy, he was always getting high. The first few months in the beginning of my pregnancy, I seemed to be going through a lot of withdrawals from coming down instantly off the drugs and alcohol. That's why I became so sick at the start of my pregnancy. I had to force myself to quit. With God giving me the strength to do so. I was emotional and being high-risk made all the complications that could affect me and my baby much worse in my case. After 3 days of feeling depressed I decided to go back to try and settle things out with Brandon. The next day after that, doctor Sue Jackson had called to set the date for inducing me. Labor induction is the process or treatment that stimulates childbirth and delivery. Labor inducing is recommended by the doctor when the woman or the baby's health is at high risk of complications. My baby was expected to arrive in early fall of October. It was now September. I had one more month to prepare for the arrival of my child. I set up the baby's crib and organized the room for my baby. I was so excited and nervous at the same time. I stood by my baby's window in the room with my head bowed down to pray one last prayer before the special day of delivery. I had asked God once more to keep my baby safe and healthy no matter what happens to me.

(James 1:17-18) "Every good and perfect gift is from above, coming down from the Father of the heavenly lights, who does not change like shifting shadows, He chose to give us birth through the word of truth, that we might be a kind of firstfruits of all he created."

Children are truly a gift from God. It is a blessing that we should always cherish with love. The day came and I was as ready as I could be. I was nervous and scared on my way to the hospital. Brandon's mom was very supportive along with my mom. Even though my mom and I had our differences, she was still very supportive. They were all on their way to meet me at the hospital. Trinity came as well after having her baby 2 months ago. She to tried to be supportive with her just curious to know if the baby was actually Brandon's or not. Little did I know, she was still not the friend I thought she was. Trinity, my mom and Brandon's mom all supported me into the delivery room because I was a young teenager about to give birth. I felt that I needed as much support as possible at the time. We all then arrived at University hospital. I met up with doctor Sue Jackson. She then took me back to the labor and delivery unit for my induction. Everyone then followed after. Soon after induction I felt pain I have never felt before. I soon started screaming and Trinity ran to get the nurse. Trinity had told me the nurse would soon be in to start an epidural treatment. An epidural is an injection in your back to stop the feeling of pain during labor. This creates numbness from the bellybotton on down. This allows a woman to be alert and awake still throughout labor with the feeling of pressure. There are three stages of labor contractions, childbirth and the delivery of the placenta. The first stage is when the uterus starts to contract and then relax. The ability to feel pressure enables the woman to push when the time comes to allowing the woman to give birth, this is called second stage labor. Following after is the third stage which is pushing out the placenta that is attached to the baby's umbilical cord. Soon after the first stage of my labor began the second stage had followed. Then the doctor began telling me its time to push after checking my cervix for dilation. I felt painful pressure while pushing. I began having a seizure during delivery.   Trinity ran to grab the nurses as they began putting oxygen over my face. The nurses quickly snapped me out of my seizure. I was still In the middle of delivery. The seizure lasted about only 2 minutes. I then resumed pushing as I was screaming. The baby then began crowning. My strength was slowly leaving me as the doctor was saying that my baby's face was turning blue. It didn't seem like I was pushing hard enough. The seizure I had made me very weak. I was just barely with it. The doctor used a tool to cut by the vaginal opening to allow the baby to slide out. They then took the baby and cleaned him up. They started a brief oxygen treatment on him since he was turning blue. I soon heard the beautiful sound of my baby's first cry. This brought tears of joy to my heart. I felt blessed! I had so much love for my child that I was determined to give him a life that he deserved. I had a beautiful, healthy baby boy. His name was Andrew Thomas Lockwood.

(1 Samuel 1:27) "For this child I prayed, and the Lord has granted me my request which I asked of him."

I felt that this was a journey to a new beginning in my life.

Chapter 12
The Journey to A New Beginning
(Part One)

In Fall of 2009, God had given me the blessings and joys of motherhood. I felt blessed to have my newborn son which was truly a gift from above. The love of being a mother was such a beautiful thing.

(Proverbs 31:25) "She is clothed with strength and dignity, and she laughs without fear of the future."

I was indeed a young mother caring for my precious child who was so sweet, innocent and pure in the sight of the Lord. With his sweet, kind, and gentle eyes always staring back at me, was beyond measure. This was truly the first time I had experienced such joy and happiness. Despite all the traumatic events that had occurred in my life, the love I shared with my son was so precious to me. I was willing to go above and beyond for my child. I have been sober for quite some time now. My grandparents came by the apartment one day to see my newborn son after we came home from the hospital. It was such a joy to them that they were great-grandparents now. That brought tears of joy and happiness into their hearts. Brandon and I took a trip up to New York for a few days to visit Brandon's family. They wanted to meet our new baby boy Andrew. Things were starting to turn around for the better, so I thought. One late afternoon after returning from our trip to New York, TJ came by the apartment to hangout with Brandon. I was laying the baby down in his crib when by curiosity I began to smell a very familiar smell coming from the kitchen. I walked in the kitchen after laying the baby down, there I found TJ and Brandon smoking by the kitchen window. I then lost my temper. I then began to scream and shout at them telling them to get out. I was willing to be a very protective mama bear. I did not want anything like that around my son. At this point Brandon and I were getting into a lot of face to face arguments. I started getting frustrated with Brandon and his friends. I had told him we needed to both start working to provide for our son. He then got a job working as a vendor downtown. I decided I was going to beg for my job back at the club. I knew I had made so much money in the past working there. I wanted nothing more than to provide for my child. I found out the girl I got into with the last time I worked there had quit months ago. I apologized with sincerity to the security guy about my behavior. He considered giving me my job back. I had stopped breastfeeding after a month then began working back at the nightclub. I was back to doing some drinking and smoking. I stayed away from the heavy drugs. I drank and smoked at the club. I didn't want that stuff around my son. Sometimes I would go upstairs to the attic or outside away from everyone to drink and smoke cigarettes away from the baby. Brandon and I were arguing a lot more. My mind couldn't take it anymore! I had ended our relationship. We still lived together for a period of time.

(Psalms 68:6) "Those who are without friends, God puts in families; he makes free those who are in chains; but those who are turned away from him are given a dry land."

I felt lonely and unloved. I felt abandoned by my close friends. My mind was so focused on providing for my child. I wanted to give him the love and the family that he deserved. My faith was still weak. My hope was almost lost. I felt eager to start a new relationship after ending my relationship with Brandon. One night at the club I was talking to a guy named Johnathan. We exchanged numbers that night. He seemed nice until I went back with him to his place that night. I found out he was into smoking heavy drugs. He lived in a drug house with a few other people. I told myself I couldn't go back to that for the sake of my child. I lost interest in Jonathan after that night. Then I decided to deleted his number from my phone. Days later I met a guy named Derick. He seemed nice, and charming in the beginning. Then he ghosted me for a period of time. I then suddenly lost interest. I was just hoping and praying at this point, for God to send me the perfect guy to help raise my son. A guy who would also love me with a love thats so real and true. That was all I had ever wanted was just someone to love me. A man who wouldn't hurt me or take advantage of how I was taken advantage of in the past. I wanted someone I could trust and depend on to share my life with, just like in a Cinderella story.

(1 Corinthians 13:4-7) "Love is patient and kind; love does not envy or boast; it is not arrogant or rude, it does not insist on its own way; it is not irritable or resentful; it does not rejoice in wrongdoing, but rejoices with the truth. Love bears all things, believes all things, hopes all things endures all things."

Love is everlasting because God is love and he is everlasting in his gift of love for all mankind. God sent his one and only son to die for our sins out of great love in Jesus Christ our Lord. He has given us many gifts like faith, hope and love. With all the pain I've suffered through it was hard to trust anyone anymore. I soon felt depressed again. I had begun to drink and smoke a lot more. I wanted all the pain to just go away that I was feeling deep inside myself. I wanted to trust in the Lord I just didn't quite know just yet. I was once again living according to my flesh.

Chapter 13
The Journey to A New Beginning (Part Two)

It was the beginning of spring in the year of 2010. I was still working at the club. One night, I was working with my friend Elena. She had just started working at the club after breaking up with her boyfriend whom she was living with. Now, she is living with one of her friends. It started out like any other night. This night became so unexpected when I met a man named Ralph Fidelis. Elena was introduced to Ralph's friend Chase. I was sitting at the bar that night having some drinks with Elena. Ralph walked over toward the bar to sit down right next to me. He introduced himself to me as Ralph Fidelis. Then we began to conversate and laugh. I have to admit he seemed quite funny in his own comical way with his sarcasm. Things seemed to be going well. Although with all the trauma in my past,

I knew in my mind that this was too good to be true. He seemed like such a gentleman walking me out to my car late at night. He insisted I got to my car safely. I just wasn't use to someone like that. I'm so use to getting hurt by guys all the time. I didn't know how to respond to what seemed like such a good kind hearted man. I walked away at first with a whatever attitude. In my heart I felt like I couldn't trust anyone. Jesus explains:

(John 8:44) "You are of the father the devil, and your will is to do your fathers desires, he was a murderer from the beginning, and does not stand in the truth, because there is no truth in him. When he lies, he speaks out of his own character, for he is a liar and the father of lies."

The devil is a liar and will stop at nothing to corrupt and confuse our minds. He turns us away from the truth which is in Christ Jesus. The devil's motive is to create chaos and confusion. He looks at the opposite from what is good in our life. In this moment it was hard for me to understand that God had answered my prayer about sending me someone who truly loves, cares, and would not hurt me. The whispers from the evil spirits inside my mind were telling me, I would be alone raising my child for the rest of my life. I was still struggling with some deep depression and high levels of anxiety caused by the tramatic events that took place throughout my life. Anxiety and deppression is also caused by evil spirits. I had told Ralph about my son Andrew. He wanted to continue to talk to me and get to know more about my son and I, so we exchanged numbers. We began texting each other back and forth every night for the past month. I realized, as I said to myself, how can this man be actually interested in someone like me? I had no confidence in myself or God at this time. I felt so insecure of myself that it was hard to let someone else into my heart.

(1 John 4:7) "Beloved, let us love one another, for love is from God, and whoever loves has been born of God and knows God."

I wanted to learn how to love God's way. I had to start by trusting in God since God is love. We then met up outside of the club on our first real date to the IX indoor amusement park. Ralph got the chance to meet my son Andrew. I didn't realize at this point that Ralph fell in love with my son the minute he laid eyes on him, wanting to raise him as his own with me by my side. It was like a father and son connection. Andrew was only six months old when we ment Ralph.

(Romans 12:9) "Love must be sincere, hate what is evil, cling to what is good."

God can reveal things to us through divine intervention and guidance, whether it's through a sermon, advice from a trusted mentor, friend, or even an unexpected encounter with someone. I didn't realize at this time that God had plans for me and Andrew to be in Ralph's life. I was still in so much doubt of myself. To be with someone like the gentleman that Ralph was, It was just too good to be true. I had to not only learn to trust in the Lord with all the plans he had for me, I also needed to learn to let go of my past in order to have more peace in my life. That was very difficult for me at that time because of all the trauma I experienced throughout my life.

(Isaiah 43:18-19) "Forget the former things; do not dwell on the past. See, I am doing a new thing! Now it springs up; do you not perceive it? I am making a way in the desert and streams in the wasteland."

God can change us wholeheartedly when we let go of the strongholds of our past. We can rely on Jesus when we get tempted to remember the traumas of our past. I had to learn to rely on Christ. I needed to have more faith in his word. I was listening to my own rather than the spirit of God that I didn't realize was dwelling within me when I accepted Christ as my Lord and Savior. My faith was not good. I had very little faith in Lord. I struggled a lot with trust. Ralph seemed like a good guy. He had a good head on his shoulders. He was a hard working man. He enjoyed the company of being around my son and I. One night I spent the night at Ralph's place. Then the next morning I got a phone call from Brandon saying our friend TJ had got killed in a drunk driving accident which brought me on my knees asking God why or how could this of happened? I didn't understand at this point, everything that was suddenly happening. I didn't want to deal with another loss in my life. I was deeply heart stricken when I heard the news about TJ's death. Brandon and I were close friends with TJ. Brandon had mentioned while still on the phone with him, that we were getting evicted. Which made me speechless, since Brandon and I were no longer together and I had nowhere to go. My emotions were all over the place. I immediately quit my job at the nightclub. I was so upset I just couldn't mentally handle everything that was going on. I felt worried because here I am a young single mother taking care of a 6 month old baby with no place to go. Jesus says:

(Matthew 6:34) "Therefore do not worry about tomorrow, for tomorrow will worry about itself. Each day has enough trouble of its own."

This verse teaches us that our focus should be on the present, not worrying about the past or about tomorrow. God wants us to be present in the here and now, knowing that He will take care of our

future as our Jehovah Jireh our provider. I had to
focus more on trusting the Lord rather than my flesh.
I had sent Andrew over to my mom's place until I
could figure out what my living situation was going
to look like. Even though my mom and I had our
disagreements with each other, she still wanted to be
there for her grandson. I later learned that Brandon
was hanging out with Trinity at the bars, when I was
away hanging out with Ralph. Not that I really
cared since we were no longer together. I still felt
deceived since she was my friend and Brandon was
the father of my child. Trinity came by after hearing
about my situation from Brandon the day we were
supposed to be evicted out of mine and Brandon's
apartment. She then offered me to stay with her. I
was skeptical at first since I had a long history with
Trinity. We had our differences from that last time I
lived with her. I felt a sense of relief knowing my
son would have a roof over his head. I decided to
move in once again with Trinity. I began moving
my stuff into the basement of her place. I then saw
Ralph pulling up in his SUV in Trinity's driveway

where I told him I was now staying. Ralph got out of his car to approach me saying that he wanted to know if my son and I would like to stay with him instead. He told me he didn't trust Trinity. He seemed to suspect before I was aware that Trinity was not a good friend. Deep down I knew Trinity was no good for me. She was a liar and a deceiver. I never really understood why I kept going back to her friendship, I just did.

(Jeremiah 9:5-9) "Beware of your friends; do not trust anyone in your clan. For every one of them is a deceiver, and every friend a slanderer. Friend deceives friend, and no one speaks the truth. They have taught their tongues to lie; they weary themselves with sinning."

Some people like Trinity appear to seem wise on the outside. On the inside they only wish evil upon others which is a great sin in the eyes of the Lord. Have you ever had a friend like Trinity who has done you so wrong? Trinity was like a magnet pulling me back towards her lies and manipulation. The evil spirits that were attached to Trinity were trying to take full control over me. In time I had to learn that some people in my life were not worth holding onto. The devil is indeed a liar. He can manipulate through people that are not godly people, nor recognizing the truth that is through Jesus Christ. I had to learn forgiveness, trust, love, and patience by moving forward in my life.

(Galatians 5:22-25) "But the fruit of the Spirit is love, joy, peace, patience, kindness, goodness, faithfulness, gentleness, self-control; against such things there is no law. And those who belong to Christ Jesus have crucified the flesh with its passions and desires. If we live by the Spirit, let us also walk by the Spirit."

I needed God to help me to start walking more in the spirit and not of my flesh. By doing so I had to set my mind focused on Him. I needed to move on from my past to start relying on God more to plan a new direction for my life. Ralph then explained to me that he had a spare room for my son and I and he had plenty of space to store all my stuff. I was so confused and worried at first because I didn't know if I could trust him or not. I needed guidance from the Lord. I just didn't understand how to trust yet. So many times I've been hurt, lied to with great deception and deceit. I just felt like I couldn't trust anyone any more. My spirit was very broken. I willing to try to trust the plans that God had for me. I went with Ralph whom I only knew for about a month. I was hoping and praying that everything will work out according to God's will for me. I then told Trinity about my new motive in moving in with Ralph. Secretly she had her own motive and attitude with all this. She seemed a little aggravated at first with her whatever like I care attitude. I told her I was leaving with Ralph. Then she acted calm about it. Ralph began to help me load mine and Andrews belongings into his SUV. He was helping me grab everything I had just stored in Trinity's basement. I then thought to myself, this may be a new beginning in my life that God had planned for me. I didn't know where this road would go. I just knew I had to see God through it, by trusting his plans for me. I

had a lot to learn through my journey. I was willing
to try a fresh start with my life.

*(2 Corinthians 5:7) "Therefore, if anyone is in Christ, he
is a new creation. The old has passed away; behold, the new
is here!"*

Everyone anticipates a new beginning which simply
means letting go of the past and looking forward
toward a new future.

Chapter 14
Experiencing Tragic Loss

It was April of 2010 when our dear friend TJ was tragically taken in death by a drunk driving accident.

(Ephesians 5:18) "And do not get drunk with wine, for that is debauchery, but be filled with the spirit."

According to this verse the word debauchery means excessive indulgence in sensual pleasures. This is a great sin that is mentioned as an immoral sin in the bible. It was said that TJ was on his way to come see Brandon before his death had occurred. Even though Brandon and I had ended our relationship we were both heart broken to hear what had happened. The police had met and talked with Brandon about the incident. He and I had no clue that TJ had made plans to come see Brandon after leaving the bar with his friends that night. We were told by the police that he was driving with two other people in the car while intoxicated. His friend Desmond who had also died on impact, and a girl named Raquel that was in the backseat who had survived with some bruises, fractured bones and a concussion. The police had questioned her at the hospital when she was finally able to speak. Before they could set a funeral date the police had to investigate everything that went on that night leading up to the car crash as to how and why it happened, and were drugs involved? Of course TJ was a drug dealer and the police found a 10 ounce bag of marjuana in the middle compartment of TJ's car. The penalties for drinking and driving, and adding to that, the possession of illegal drugs can include misdemeanors to felony offenses, which can also include fines and jail time. The police focused their attention on Raquel because she was the only one who had survived the crash. Later on we had discovered that Raquel was the only one in the car that was wearing her seatbelt. The police had charged Raquel with only a misdemeanor. She had some fines to pay, along with some jail time. She was intoxicated and charged with disorderly conduct. They charged her with possession of drugs that the police had found in the car. The bible tells us over and over again that sin leads to death and destruction, because there are consequences with our actions regarding how God designed us to live and obey him. If were living by the flesh and not being lead by the spirit of God, sin can cause an internal conflict with God and ourselves. This can lead to health issues by taking a physical toll on your body such as an illness, or pain, or even physical or mental damage that may be permanent or temporary. As a result of original sin, human nature is weakened in its powers, subject to ignorance, suffering and the domination of death, and inclined to sin. In the bible Paul explains:

(Romans 5:12-21) "Therefore, just as sin came into the world through one man, and death spread to all men because all sinned, for sin indeed was in the world before the law was given, but sin is not counted where there is no law. Yet death reigned from Adam to Moses, even over those whose sinning was not like the transgression of Adam, who was a type of

the one was to come. But the free gift is not like the
trespass. For if many died through one man's trespass, much
more have the grace of God and the free gift by the grace of
that one man Jesus Christ abounded for many. And the free
gift is not like the result of that one man's sin. For the
judgement following one trespass brought condemnation, but
the free gift following many trespasses brought justification.
For if, because of one man's trespass, death reigned through
one man, much more will those who receive the abundance of
grace and the free gift of righteousness reign in life through
the one man Jesus Christ. Therefore, as one trespass led to
condemnation for all men, so one act of righteousness leads to
justification and life for all men. For as by the one man's
disobedience the many were made sinners, so by the one
man's obedience the many will be made righteous. Now the
law came in to increase the trespass, but where sin increased,
grace abounded all the more, so that, as sin reigned in death,
grace also might reign through righteousness leading to
eternal life through Jesus Christ our Lord."

This explains the comparison between Adam and
Jesus. Adam sinned and this was how death entered
the world. However, it was not the law, but Jesus
who gave his life for this purpose eliminated what
Adam did. Jesus's death not only cancelled the harm
caused by Adam's fall, but surpasses it by far. We
all have consequences for our sins we commit in life
that we have to pay for, however; if we acknowledge
our wrong doings in accepting the love of Christ in
our life, he will forgive us of those sins. As time
went pass, soon the investigation had ended. The
date was set for TJ's funeral. Even though I started a
new relationship with Ralph, he was very
understanding about the situation. I then
accompanied Brandon to TJ's funeral. I could tell
Brandon was broken inside and confused about
everything that had happened to TJ. I became very
emotional as we pulled into the parking lot of the
funeral home where it was time for the wake.
Brandon was nervous and emotional, so we did the
only thing we could think of at this time to numb the
pain. We began smoking a blunt to get high in

Brandon's car before going inside. Afterwards; we then made our way inside the funeral home. As we entered inside the building, we saw TJ's mother at the foot of his casket. She began to cry her eyes out with tears running on the sides of both her cheeks. Her head was faced down over TJ's casket. She grabbed her son's lifeless hand in devastation while falling onto her knees. It became such a sad and very emotional time for everyone. My heart really went out towards TJ's mom. No mother should ever have to bury her child. Sadly the mother of our Lord Jesus had to do the same thing after his death on the cross. Jesus's mother had to watch him suffer while she stood at the cross along with Jesus's beloved friend and disciple whom he loved.

(John 19:25-27) "But standing by the cross of Jesus were his mother and his mother's sister, Mary the wife of Clopas, and Mary Magdalene. When Jesus saw his mother and the disciple whom he loved standing nearby, he said to his mother, "Woman, behold, your son!" Then he said to the

disciple, "Behold, your mother!" And from that hour the

disciple took her to his own home."

Jesus wanted his friend John to comfort Mary in her hour of need. In this dark hour, all this was a lot to take in for everyone. It was very emotional for Brandon and I. Brandon then walked up to TJ's mother to give her a hug. I surrounded her with my arms wide open to show her love and sympathy for her loss, and for the loss of our friend TJ. Soon after that emotional moment Brandon and I stepped outside with some of our other friends. They were also friends with TJ that wanted to smoke and get high. Getting high with Brandon and his other friends may have numbed the pain, but it doesn't take away the pain. I had a hard time understanding how or why that happened the way it did with TJ. My journey of the faith continued with lessons that I still had yet to learn. My first lesson was how to learn to continue to trust God's plans for me.

Chapter 15
Spiritual Awakening

After our final farewells, Brandon and I went our separate ways. I then called Ralph to come pick me up from the cemetery where they had laid TJ to his final resting place. While waiting for Ralph to come pick me up I decided to take a stroll around the cemetery while smoking a cigarette still trying to wrap my head around everything. I was emotional from the loss of TJ. I felt overwhelmed with the eviction. I was stressed about moving in with a guy I've only been dating for a month in a half. I didn't know if I could trust him or not.

(Philippians 4:6-7) "Be anxious for nothing, but in everything by prayer and supplication, with thanksgiving, let your requests be made known to God; and the peace of God, which surpasses all understanding, will guard your hearts and minds through Christ Jesus."

I felt the need to start trusting more in the Lord rather than my own self ego that is of the flesh. My prayer life was not at my fullest just yet. I loved the Lord so much I was ready to give Him my full heart. The Lord wants us whole heartedly. I just felt like I needed more assurance. There were moments I still felt depressed with some anxiety. Minutes later, Ralph pulled up into the parking lot in his SUV near the cemetery. We had all of mine and Andrew's belongings packed up in the car. We were ready to finally move into Ralph's place. We also had to go pick up Andrew from my mom's house. My mom had Andrew for a month while I was going through all these series of unfortunate events with Brandon. She was not happy about hearing I was moving in with a man I only knew for a few months. I was a little skeptical at first my self. Ralph was very supportive. He assured me that my son was going to be in a safe environment with all the necessary things provided for him. Ralph lived in a duplex on the second floor from his mom on the eastside of Cleveland where he grew up. We pulled up next to the house. We then began unloading the car with our belongings. We made our way to the entrance of Ralph's house. We were then greeted by Ralph's mom Shirley. She offered to watch Andrew while Ralph and I unpacked mine and Andrew's things. We started to get Andrew's crib all set up in his new room. We were trying to get things settled in Ralph's place realizing there was more stuff to be brought in from the car. Going back to the car we gathered more boxes of our belongings. We then headed towards the stairs back to Ralph's unit. As we began walking up the stairs, I noticed some strange writings on the wall. It was written in black permanent marker leading up towards the door to Ralph's unit. I wondered what they ment or why they were there. I then got curious and asked Ralph what the writings on the wall were. He said that his niece was sleepwalking one night and in a trance. She had started writing what she was shown in a dream she had one night. The dream she had was of a spirit board called an ouija board that had letters and numbers. The spirit inside the dream had communicated with her through the ouija board in the dream. The spirit in the dream started communicating with her. She then started writing the symbols shown in her dream then began to write them on the wall. Ouija boards are said to be used in communication with the dark spirits of this world. The demonic can possess non-believers and taunt them in their dreams.

(Matthew 12:43-45) "When the unclean spirit has gone out of a person, it passes through waterless places seeking rest, but finds none. Then it says, I will return to my house from which I came. And when it comes, it finds the house empty, swept, and put in order. Then it goes and brings with it seven other spirits more evil than itself, and they enter and dwell there, and the last state of that person is worse than the first. So also will it be with this evil generation."

This explains the use of the unclean spirit. This is a timely reminder that in the spiritual realm there is a spiritual warfare going on in and around us. That includes the work of malign spirits seeking to defile us and therefore defeat us on our walk with God.

This reminds us that whenever we turn to God, we need to focus our minds on seeking Him on our journey of faith. Evil can be conquered by the power that is in Christ Jesus. I felt dark forces at hand all around me in this place. Ralph continued to work on fixing Andrew's room up while I unpacked my things. I started unpacking some of my dishes in the kitchen that belonged to my aunt that passed away. I noticed another other than the one we came in at. I began to get curious so I asked Ralph about it. He said it was a door leading upstairs to the attic that his family has never used. It was starting to get late in the day so we decided to finish unpacking the rest of the boxes tomorrow. Ralph had finished setting up my baby's crib so he could go to sleep. Ralph an I decided to sit on the couch to relax and watch movies. Ralph didn't stay up super late since he had to work in the morning. Ralph worked a full-time job Monday through Friday. My first night sleeping in his house was very difficult I began having nightmares of past events. I work up in terror, with tears suddenly pouring down my face.

Ralph woke up to the sounds of my emotional crying. He was very loving with his compassion toward everything I had been through. He then wrapped his arms around me as I began to fall back asleep while he held me close to him.

(Psalm 128:2) "You will definitely enjoy what you've worked hard for- you'll be happy; and things will go well for you."

God rewards those who work hard. He shows mercy for those who are compassionate towards others.

(Psalm 21:2) "You have given him his heart's desire and have not withheld the request of his lips."

Ralph always wanted a love to share. He hoped and prayed that one day he would be able to find a woman to share his life with. Ralph was soon falling in love with me. I was so hung up on my past traumas that I didn't even realize Ralph's love for me. I just seemed to keep pushing him away. With all the hurt I've been through in my past it was hard for me to open my self to trusting someone. In time God would soon guide me to the right path perhaps

that path leads to a spiritual awaking. One morning
after Ralph left for work, I woke up to a strange
scratching sound near the attic door. It startled me
so I began inspecting where it was coming from. As
I made my way toward the attic door I then began
hearing a loud knock that frightened me. I grabbed
Andrew and stormed down the stairs towards
Shirley's door. At the knock of the door Ralph's
mom Shirley saw Andrew and I standing at the
doorway with great fear and worriness in our eyes.
She kindly took us in and told me that Andrew and I
were always welcome down here while Ralph was at
work. Shirley's husband Frank was very friendly
and loved Andrew with a passion. Andrew soon
recognized Shirley and Frank as grandma and
grandpa. I felt a sense of safety and secureness
when I was around Ralph's parents. One night after
Ralph had come home from work I had told him
about the noises I had been hearing. He explained
to me that a little girl was haunting his house after
she had died previously before Ralph and his family
moved into the house. He then explained the tragic

story of how the little girl had died. He said her life was tragically taken in the early 1970's in a hit and run accident while running into the street after her ball. He said one time he saw the little girl looking at him through the window that was two stories up from the ground. In our christian faith we're taught that a person's spirit cannot wander the earth because the spirit of a human belongs to God since the beginning of time. According to the bible it says:

> (Genesis 2:7) "Then the LORD God formed the man of dust from the ground and breathed into his nostrils the breath of life, and the man became a living creature."
>
> (Ecclesiastes 12:7) "Then shall the dust return to the earth as it was: and the spirit shall return unto God who gave it."

Ralph and his family lived in the house since he was in his early teens. In 1995 Ralph's parents took ownership of the house. Ralph told me that his ancestors used to practice witchcraft in the early 1800's. The house he grew up in as a child on Fleet

avein the early 1980's was also haunted with
demonic spirits. These demonic spirits seemed to be
following him from place to place from his family
history in witchcraft.

*(Numbers 14:18) "The Lord is slow to anger, abounding
in love and forgiving sin and rebellion. Yet he does not leave
the guilty unpunished; he punishes the children for the sin of
the parents to the third and fourth generation."*

Evil spirits can attach themselves through a line of
generations. This is called a generational curse. A
generational curse involves the lack of love for God
throughout generations, because of acts of evil
throughout our bloodline. For unbelievers this
allows various openings for dark spirits to enter in,
to torment us throughout generations until God is
once again acknowledged through his son Jesus.
Dark spirits that roam the earth often like to torment
people. Although they sometimes seem to act in
good ways.

*(2 Corinthians 11:14) "Even Satan disguises himself as
an angel of light."*

God the Father sent his one and only son Jesus to save us from the powers of darkness as he himself overcame the evil's of this world by the power of his death and resurrection. One day I heard a loud noise coming from the attic. It sounded like someone bouncing a basketball across the room. I jumped out of bed with concern on my face. I went to grab Andrew when I realized he disappeared from his crib. I ran in panic downstairs to get Shirley's attention after banging on her door out of worry for my son. We began to search around the house for him. In a panic I began to ask God in prayer for help in search of my son to let him be found. The house was quiet. We searched for nearly an hour. Shirley and I decided to double search again around his crib. There we found Andrew sound asleep surrounded by all his stuffed animals in his stuffed animal bin. I began thanking God with all my heart as I worried for my son's safety. He looked like a little cabbage patch doll! Later we found out he crawled out of bed and landed safely with his soft, fluffy stuffed animals. He feel asleep while snuggling with them.

Shirley and I began to tell Frank and Ralph about the whole thing. They were relieved that we had found him. I kept thanking God that day for keeping my son safe. Then one night I was having a nightmare which had occurred for many nights in a row. In my dream I saw myself walking toward the attic door as something was calling me towards it. I had this dream almost every night. Then one night I felt a dark demonic presence hovering over me. I felt it holding me down as if something heavy was placed on my chest. In that moment I could not move any of my limbs. It was as if it felt like my body was stiff and could not move. My eyes were wide open in much fear. Then I had felt a dark force of some kind breathing very heavily against my face.

(Psalm 55:3) "Because of the voice of the enemy, because of the pressure of the wicked; for they bring down trouble upon me and in anger they bear a grudge against me."
We should be well-aware of the various ways in which satan works. He attacks believers when he thinks it will be to his advantage. Of course Satan

tries to attack us. He wants nothing more than to see us fail.

(2 Corinthians 2:11) "So that we would not be outwitted by Satan; for we are not ignorant of his designs."

Satan doesn't want to see us grow in God's kingdom. Prayer is a powerful strategy to defeat satan and his minions in our lives and to recognize his attacks. As we expect these attacks we must be ready to fight them with the truth of God's word. I wanted to scream that night but something was preventing me from using my voice.

(Mark 9:25) And when Jesus saw that a crowd came running together, he rebuked the unclean spirit, saying it, "You mute and deaf spirit, I command you, come out of him and never enter him again."

As believers we have authority our the devil. Jesus gave us that perfect example by sending us his Holy Spirit within us when we are born again believers baptized in the spirit. Baptized in the spirit indicates recognized the fullness of the Holy Spirit. Being filled with the Holy spirit means you have that power and authority over the enemy. I felt my faith begin to grow, the more I begged God to save me from the attacks of the evil that was lurking around. One morning I went downstairs to visit with Frank and Shirley. I asked to use her computer. Shirley and Frank watched Andrew for me. I was looking for job's on Shirley's computer. God guided me to a new purpose in my life. I took an interest in working in the healthcare field. God's new plan for me was going to college studying healthcare. I got enrolled in a college that was near me. I began working part time in the group homes while traveling throughout Northeast Ohio and going to school. Ralph lended his vehicle to me whenever I needed it. Shirley would watch Andrew for me while I was working and going to school. Frank agreed to help Shirley watch Andrew. Frank offered to help with homework assignments. He even offered to help me study for all my upcoming exams. God had big plans for my life. This was my time to trust God more for the plans he had for me. The Lord had so much more instored for me in my life with Ralph. My spirit was willing but my flesh was still weak.

(Mark 9:23-24) Jesus said unto them "If you can believe, all things are possible to him who believes." Immediately the father of the child cried out and said with tears, "Lord, I believe; help my unbelief!"

Chapter 16
The Proposal

It was toward the end of 2010 Ralph and I have
been dating for one year. Ralph and his family all
came together to celebrate Andrew's first birthday.
Andrew just turned a year old. Shirley and Frank
had enjoyed every moment. Frank and Shirley loved
having Andrew as their own grandson. Frank loved
to play funny games to have fun with him. It
warmed their hearts to see a loving smile on
Andrew's face. Andrew went to town eating and
wearing his smash cake all over his face. These
days it was truly a blessing watching my son take his
first steps. Jesus said:

(Matthew 19:14) "Let the little children come to me."
As parents growing in faith we long to see our
children in their firsts in everything like their first
smile, first time crawling, first steps, first tooth, first
haircut, first loose tooth. It is our desire as parents
in the faith to walk with our children as they take

their first steps toward Jesus. Children are so pure and innocent in the eyes of the Lord. I wanted to be the loving, caring mother to my son. I longed to help give him the life he so deserved with the Lord guiding my steps in the spirit. Ralph loved Andrew with a passion that Brandon felt he could not give. I learned that he moved to New York to be near his family. After Brandon left I really didn't hear much from him anymore from this point on. My love for Ralph grew as we walked closer with the Lord. Ralph was new in understanding my christian background. He was willing to learn as his love for me grew deeper. In the summer of 2011, Ralph and I decided to take Andrew down to Miami Florida to meet his grandfather Louie for the first time. I then called my dad to tell him the good news about coming down to Florida to meet his new one and only grandchild. My dad felt so delighted to see Andrew. He couldn't wait to see me again. I couldn't wait to see him! My dad and I built a great relationship over the years since the first day we met. God connected us to meet and grow to know each other more and more as a father should know his children.

(Malachi 4:6) "And he will turn the hearts of fathers to their children and the hearts of children to their fathers, lest I come and smite the land with a curse."

The fathers in this scripture represent our dead ancestors who died without the privilege of receiving the gospel. God calls us to be his people through Jesus. Many get invited to come to know Jesus; only few accept him as Lord.

(Matthew 22:14) "For many are called, but few are chosen."

Ralph and I drove down to Miami from Cleveland. We stayed with my dad at his house. We arrived at my dads house in Miami. He then came outside to greet us with love and hugs. He was so happy to see Andrew and I. He met Ralph whom I had been dating for a year. It seemed like Ralph and my dad didn't always agree with each other. They both shared their love for Andrew and I. In time my dad and Ralph learned to get along. We enjoyed our time at Miami beach with all of us together as family. Ralph and my dad helped me cover

Andrew's feet in sand. That didn't work out very well since the sand was tickling Andrew's toes. Then we decided to bury Ralph in the sand. My dad and I enjoyed drinking bahama mama's while laying in the sun. Ralph was enjoying his time building sandcastles with Andrew. All of us enjoyed hearing the sound of the ocean waves while feeling the cool ocean breeze with the ocean shore waves hitting our feet.

(Psalms 23:1-3) "The Lord is my shepherd; I shall not want. He makes me lie down in green pastures. He leads me beside the still waters. He restores my soul. He leads me in paths of righteousness for his name's sake."

These first 3 verses of Psalm 23 reminds us that the good shepard takes care of his sheep and that shepard is Jesus. These verses describe the wisdom, strength and kindness of our God. God is good and worthy of our trust all the time. Sometimes it's hard for us to trust in God to our fullest when our human nature gets the best of us. Throughout our journey of faith the Lord guides us through the Holy Spirit,

drawing us closer on our walk with him. I felt a
sense of happiness deep inside being with my son,
my dad and Ralph. I felt a happiness I thought I
could never have. God had given me the gift of
motherhood, the love from a father. God gave me
the gift of a compassionate love between Ralph and
I. After our day at the beach, my dad cooked dinner
at his house. He cooked some delicious meals. We
watched some movies till we decided to go to bed to
get ready for the next day. Then the next day Ralph
and I decided to take some time to ourselves. My
dad offered to watch my son as we headed off to the
beach together. As we arrived, we began to stroll
alongside the ocean shores of the beach while
holding hands. It was very comforting walking on
the beach on our bare feet, feeling the sand between
our toes while the waves hit our feet along the shore
line. We decided to write our names in the sand
together. As we finished writing our names in the
sand it said; "Ralph and Grace together forever."
We both looked at each other with a heart warming
smile. We could feel the love building for each other

as God intended for us. As the sunset came and the beach became less cluttered with people, Ralph got down on one knee as he then suddenly grabbed my hand and said these words, "Grace will you marry me?" Of course, I was surprised! I felt like I must of been dreaming when I heard those words. I was very much awake filled with tears of joy running down my face as I said yes to Ralph. In that moment my ultimate prayer was answered. I was finally going to have the man of my dreams that I had been asking God for. I thanked God for giving my son a father that he deserves. I believed that God intended for all this to happen for me. I thanked God that day for giving me Ralph to be apart of mine and Andrew's life. We left the beach and returned back to my dads house telling him the good news. He seemed happy for the both of us as a father should when their child gets engaged.

(Romans 12:9-10) "Love must be sincere. Hate what is evil; cling to what is good. Be devoted to one another in love. Honor one another above yourselves."

Being engaged made me realize what it means to be truly in love with someone. I felt my relationship with Ralph growing more deeper in love. It couldn't have been for a more kind-hearted respectful man like Ralph. I felt like God gave the perfect man for me and my son. We soon said our farewells to my dad and kept in touch. We then started to make our way back to Ohio. With excitement we were eager to get back to tell Ralph's parents the good news. Filled with excitement we then made our way back. We then made it back to Cleveland. Ralph and I were so excited to tell Shirley and Frank the good news about our engagement. Frank and Shirley couldn't be more happy for us although we didn't have a lot of money. We just planned for a small simple wedding. One morning I overheard Frank telling Shirley how proud he was of his son for wanting to marry a kind woman like me. Frank said he was proud of Ralph for the father that he became for Andrew. I felt blessed that Andrew and I were going to be a part of Ralph's family. I had a deep love connection with Ralph's parents, as did

Andrew. One morning Frank was taken to the hospital because of some health issues that turned out worse than it seemed to be. I could soon tell that this was going to be a tough time for both Ralph and I.

(Isaiah 33:2) "O Lord, be gracious to us; we wait for you. Be our arm every morning, our salvation in the time of trouble."

Chapter 17
In Times Of Troubled Waters

It was the middle of fall in 2011, one month after Andrew's 2nd birthday. We celebrated his birthday at my moms house. My mom decided to move out closer to the church. It was more convenient for her with all her health problems. Her new house was much bigger than the house I grew up in. Ralph had ordered pizza, and a cake for Andrew's party. It warmed my heart seeing all my siblings Adam, Ruth, Lizzie, and Cory. I even got to see grandpa Clay and grandma Asa along with my aunt Donna that always tagged along with them. Gilbert even brought ice cream for everybody. Although it seemed like Gilbert and I didn't see eye to eye, he saw the mother that I had become. At that moment I finally started to see a connection with my step dad. I always just wanted that feeling of being accepted by him as his own daughter since the bond we had with Mark was gone.

It was heartwarming to see my step dad Gilbert
bonding with my son. He tried treating Andrew as
his own grandson. Having my family all together for
my son's birthday was a blessing to me. It brought
such joy to my heart that all of us were together
getting along with one another. It was difficult
celebrating Andrew's birthday with Frank in the
hospital. He's been waiting to get surgery done at the
Cleveland Clinic hospital downtown. Ralph and I
were waiting for a phone call from Shirley to see how
the surgery went. We tried making the most out of it
by trying not to stress or worry about Franks
circumstances. We enjoyed spending time with my
family to make fun loving memories together.

*(Psalms 68:6) "God sets the solitary in families; He
brings out those who are bound into prosperity; But the
rebellious dwell in a dry land."*

Family is at the center of God's plan for the happiness
and progress of his children. The bible teaches us
that God established families from the very
beginning. It shows us many examples of strong
families. It teaches us how to have a loving, happy

family through Jesus Christ. God makes a way for all of us to be part of his eternal family.

(1 John 3:1) "See what kind of love the Father has given to us, that we should be called children of God; and so we are. The reason why the world does not know us is that it did not know him."

God loves our fellowship and connection with our families as well as our brothers and sisters in Christ. He reunites us with our families as a blessing in the perfect will of God.   Meanwhile, while we were all reminiscing and having a good time at my moms house for Andrew's birthday party, Ralph had received a disturbing phone call from Shirley about Ralph's dad. Ralph stepped outside, away from the noise of the loud party. After the phone call had ended Ralph pulled me aside away from everyone to tell me we needed to go up to the hospital after the party was over. Shirley said to Ralph over the phone that Frank was in critical condition after the surgery. After a while we played games, had pizza, ate cake and ice cream. Soon we hugged everyone while saying goodbye as friends and family left the party.

We packed all Andrew's things up in Ralph's car.
Then began heading up towards the hospital where
Frank was. We arrived at the hospital to meet with
Shirley in the main lobby of the hospital. Shirley
explained to us that they had moved Frank into ICU
which means intensive care unit. An ICU handles
severe, and or potentially life threatening cases. An
intensive care unit provides the critical care and life
support for acutely ill and injured patients. Frank
was put on life support. During the surgery they
found blood clots leading up to the brain. Frank's
heart rate and oxygen levels had dropped as well.
The hospital had hooked him up to many monitors.
The nurses have been giving him medicine through
an IV. Ralph's siblings with some of his nephews all
gathered round to see Frank in his critical condition.
In that moment Ralph was having a hard time dealing
with the pain and suffering that his dad was going
through. He had to deal with the emotions of his
sisters and mother. No man ever wants to see his
mother cry. It made Ralph very upset. Shirley was so
upset seeing the sight of losing her husband. I felt

such sympathy for Ralph and his family. I wrapped
my arms around Ralph with love and sympathy for
him and his family. I allowed him to shed his tears
of sorrow on my shoulder.

*(Psalms 147:3) "He heals the broken hearted and binds
up their wounds."*

God is our comfort in our times of trouble.
Therefore it is up to us to rely on him to comfort us.
Deep down in this unpleasant time I knew God was
with us, comforting us in our times of troubled
waters. Shirley was very emotional at the thought of
losing not only a loving husband and best friend to
her, but also a good father to her children. I reached
out to my future mother in law with open arms and
hugged her close to my heart, while she began to cry
on my shoulder. The doctors and nurses came into
the room to begin taking Frank off life support.
Shirley had agreed to this procedure to be done by
signing documentation to proceed in doing so. They
then decided to move Frank to the hospice unit where
we all had followed after as they began moving him.
Hospice care is a type of health care that focuses on

the palliation of someone who is approaching the end of life. Hospice care prioritizes comfort and the quality of life by reducing pain and suffering, while attending to their emotional and spiritual needs. After he was transported to the hospice unit, we were all then told to say our final goodbyes to Frank. Shirley was so emotional while clinging on to Frank's hand. I felt in my heart the painful sorrow that she was feeling at that moment. Ralph's sisters were having a hard time dealing with their emotions of their father's long suffering, along with Ralph's brother.

(1 Thessalonians 4:13-14) "Brothers and sisters, we do not want you to be uninformed about those who sleep in death, so that you do not grieve like the rest of mankind, who have no hope. For we believe that Jesus died and rose again, and so we believe that God will bring with Jesus those who have fallen asleep in him."

Jesus is our comfort in our time of need if we just allow him to enter into our lives. He brings joy to those in their sorrows and comforts those who mourn and grieve. Jesus had moured over the loss of his dear friend Lazarus.

(John 11:35) "Jesus wept."

Jesus explains that even though we mourn we are still comforted because the Lord loves us.

(Matthew 5:4) "Blessed are they who mourn for they shall be comforted."

Soon after we all left the hospital, Frank had died. Indeed we were all mourning after that day at his memorial service. It was a hard time for us all. I came too far to give up hope I remained faithful in understanding God's will for me. I stood by Ralph and his family in their time of need with love and support. Frank was in the military. They had a special memorial service for him in honor of serving in active duty. Frank's military buddies that proudly served with Frank gave Shirley a special gift. It was a flag of the United States folded up a certain way into a triangle. Shirley was emotional with tears falling down her face. The Holy Spirit had moved in me that day to comfort Ralph and his family, with

love and tenderness in mourning with them.   The
Holy Spirit has the power to comfort all that mourn.

*(Isaiah 61:2) "To proclaim the year of the LORD's favor,
and the day of vengeance of our God; to comfort all who
mourn;*

People who experience this divine comfort describe
it as warmth, fullness, calmness, and peace. It is the
fulfillment of Jesus's promise.

*(John 14:27) "Peace I leave with you, my peace I give unto
you."*

We proceeded back to Ralph's place. Things were
quite different since Frank was gone. Soon after our
mourning had slowly come to an end, it was now
time to prepare for Ralph and I to get married.

Chapter 18
Two Becoming One

It was the beginning of the year in 2012. Ralph and I were preparing to get married. We didn't have a lot of money for a big wedding. Ralph made a vow to me that if we make it to our 10th anniversary, then he will make sure I receive the wedding that I deeply desired. I was so excited, feeling so blessed to have met Ralph. Shirley couldn't be happier for Ralph and I. She was still missing her husband Frank. She now had our wedding to look forward to. I bought a cheap 75 dollar wedding dress at the thrift store after trying it on. I couldn't believe I felt my prayers being answered. With all my heart I kept thanking God for everything he has done for me. After everything I've been through I never thought I'd be finally marrying a man that was just perfect for me.

(Matthew 17:20) "Because of your little faith, for truly I say to you, if you have faith like a grain of mustard seed, you

will say to this mountain, move from here to there and it will
move, and nothing will be impossible for you."

My faith grew more and more. I found my hope in the loving arms of the Lord. I called a few friends then tried to get in touch with my family. Grandma Asa and Grandpa Clay were under the weather. They were unable to attend the wedding. My mom was in the hospital because she had fallen and broken her leg with only a minor fracture. Adam had a new girlfriend so I didn't get to see him much. I wasn't going to allow the disappointment of my family not being there for me on my special day bring me down. I still had the support of Ralph's family and a few of our friends. We went downtown to the courthouse to pay for our marriage certificate. We planned our wedding for valentines day at tower city in downtown Cleveland. A week before the wedding we made plans for a pizza party downstairs at Shirleys place. We ordered pizza and a cheap cake at Walmart since that was all we could afford. I was nervous and excited at the same time. It seemed to all be happening so fast. God chose Ralph just for me.

(Song of Solomon 3:4) "I have found the one whom my soul loves."

I believe God gave me Ralph to be a part of mine and Andrew's life forever. I also believe He knew exactly what he was doing when Ralph and I crossed paths.

(1 Thessalonians 5:11) "Therefore encourage one another and build one another up, just as you are doing."

Relationships are all about building one another up supporting each other through good times and the bad times, no matter the circumstances. I believe God will continue to watch over both of us to see that we continue to do so. I had a hard time trusting Ralph at first. God helped me work on those trust issues and I soon started to trust more and give more of my heart. I loved Ralph with my whole heart. I prayed to God that our love and marriage would last forever. Some friends and family had their doubts about us. God had his plans for Ralph and I despite of what others have said. There was now one day

left before the wedding. I got more and more
excited. Ralph's sister soon secretly got jealous that
Ralph and I were getting married before her. Two
days ago she got her marriage license. She got
married at the courthouse to her daughter's father
that she's been with for 8 years. Ralph and I were
happy for her.

*(James 3:16) "Wherever there is jealousy and selfish
ambition, there is disorder and everything that is evil."*
Jealousy-like attitudes are driven by envy for what
others have, and an ambition to take it. The day had
come as I was out getting my hair done with my
friends Anna, Elaine, and Maria. As I looked at the
clock on my phone I realized we had to start heading
up to tower city in order to make it in time for the
wedding ceremony. I jumped in the car with Elaine
as Anna followed behind. Elaine was waiting for
Chase to come get her from the hair salon where we
were. We were on our way to tower city mall when
Ralph called in panic, wondering if everything was
ok. I assured him that I was making my way up
there with no intention of looking back on my past.

I very much wanted a new chapter of my life beginning with Ralph. God made plans for my life to spend the rest of my years with Ralph by mine and Andrew's side. I wasn't about to give that up. I trusted God's intentional unfailing love, with the plans he had for Ralph and I. Shirley called and said she made it to the mall with Andrew. We then arrived at Tower City mall. I had to take my heels off while holding my wedding dress to run in order to make it to the ceremony in time. As the ceremony was about to begin, I had just made it to the lobby where Ralph was standing beside the Judge with Chase next to him as his witness. Elaine was my witness also. The witnesses witness the ceremony, and when it's over, the witnesses witness the couple with the officiant signing the marriage license. After the short ceremony, the judge officiant said to Ralph that he may now kiss his bride. This was a new beginning for both of us when two people became one together in marriage.

(Mark 6:6-9) "But from the beginning of creation, God made them male and female. Therefore a man shall leave his

*father and mother and hold fast to his wife, and the two
shall become one flesh. So they are no longer two but one
flesh. Therefore what God has joined together, let no man
separate."*

This verse explains that two people are joined
together by God, as a man leaves his parents and
clings to his wife. I felt a sense of joy in my spirit
that day from the Lord. I felt blessed in that moment
to finally feel loved by someone who truely cared
about me. Ralph had a lot of respect for me. He
understood everything that had happened to me in
my past. I always cherished the day of my wedding.
I continued to move forward in my marriage with
Ralph trying not to look back on the things of my
past. We then headed back to Shirley's soon after.
We stopped at the park beforehand to take pictures
of Ralph and I. Our pictures are our reminder of that
day we will never forget. I loved the Lord with all
that He has done for me in my life. I felt thankful in
my heart that God sent me a man like Ralph into my
life. I knew God had even bigger plans in my life
for Ralph, my son and I. Shirley moved out to live

with Ralph's sister down in a city called Canton.
She could no longer afford the mortgage payments
on the house. It was hard for her to stay in a house
where she spent a lot of years with Frank. She felt
better to get away from the heart breaking memories
of her lost beloved husband and father of her
children. We also planned on leaving to start our
new life together while packing up all mine, Ralph's
and Andrew's stuff. We found an apartment near my
moms house.   As we finished packing the car Ralph
and I decided to go back into the house to make one
more sweep around to make sure we grabbed
everything. Suddenly I felt that dark, angry presence
surrounding me once more. It felt as if someone was
standing behind me heavily breathing down my neck
with anger. I felt the hairs on my neck standing up.
I then told Ralph we needed to hurry. The evil force
within that house was angry of our leaving.
Together we raced down the stairs out the down into
the car, with my son in my arms. Ralph followed
behind, never looking back. I encourage you who
are reading this book, don't let the devil defeat you

by stealing your joy and happiness that comes from Jesus Christ our Lord. Remember, that when you have no joy, you have no strength. That's when Satan can come in and rob you of everything you have that God already offers unto you. Satan has no refuge when the joy of the Lord is present.

(Nehemiah 8:10) "Do not grieve, for the joy of the Lord is your strength."

(Proverbs 1:5) "Let the wise hear and increase in learning, and the one who understands obtain guidance."

Dedication In Loving Memory of:

Dale Miller

I Will Remember You!

About The Author

The author Kay Williams wrote this book as a reminder that she can always trust and depend on the Lord in all circumstances. The author dedicated her book in the loving memory of Dale Miller who was a born again believer him and shared words of encouragement with her while writing her book. God used Dale to encourage the author to never give up on something that God is calling you to do. Through the eyes of Grace is a testimonial story based on true life events about the author. God has brought her out through many situations in her life. The author has found her strength in the Lord by rededication. She now attends church, and has been a member at Deliverance Christian church for quite sometime now. The author of this book is now striving to serve the Lord faithfully through the end of her days. She continues to be a light for those who still wander in darkness as an Evangelist spreading the love of Christ from one person to the next. She shows others her love for God and people by being an example through Jesus Christ. God's love is made perfect for us. Reflect on the truth that is the Word of God which is in Christ Jesus.

(Colossians 3:14) "And above all these put on love, which binds everything together in perfect harmony."

Made in the USA
Monee, IL
02 August 2023